T0171554

The Spiritual Nature of Horse

Explained by Horse

An incomparable conversation between
one exceptional horse and his human

Dante and Cathy Seabrook, D.V.M.

Veterinarian Professional Animal Communicator

BALBOA
PRESS

A DIVISION OF HAY HOUSE

ISBN: 978-1-4525-6166-0 (sc)
ISBN: 978-1-4525-6168-4 (e)
ISBN: 978-1-4525-6167-7 (hc)

Library of Congress Control Number: 2012920017

Balboa Press books may be ordered through booksellers or by contacting:

Balboa Press
A Division of Hay House
1663 Liberty Drive
Bloomington, IN 47403
www.balboapress.com
1-(877) 407-4847

Because of the dynamic nature of the Internet, any web addresses or links contained in this book may have changed since publication and may no longer be valid. The views expressed in this work are solely those of the author and do not necessarily reflect the views of the publisher, and the publisher hereby disclaims any responsibility for them.

The author of this book does not dispense medical advice or prescribe the use of any technique as a form of treatment for physical, emotional, or medical problems without the advice of a physician, either directly or indirectly. The intent of the author is only to offer information of a general nature to help you in your quest for emotional and spiritual well-being. In the event you use any of the information in this book for yourself, which is your constitutional right, the author and the publisher assume no responsibility for your actions.

Any people depicted in stock imagery provided by Thinkstock are models, and such images are being used for illustrative purposes only.
Certain stock imagery © Thinkstock.

Printed in the United States of America

Balboa Press rev. date: 11/15/2012

To all the horses I have known and loved, here and there.

Will they believe Dante?
Unless they are not with Horse, and then it matters not.

Contents

Preface...ix

Forward...xiii

Chapter 1: Normal Life in Horsedom 1

Chapter 2: Different Kinds of Horse 16

Chapter 3: Horse Families 27

Chapter 4: Foals 38

Chapter 5: Performing as Horse 48

Chapter 6: Equipment and other unmentionables.........................61

Chapter 7: Horse Senses...66

Chapter 8: Memory...77

Chapter 9: People in General...82

Chapter 10: Other Animals and Horse...96

Chapter 11: When Physical Demonstrates Spiritual 102

Chapter 12: Emotion-Biology-Mind 148

Chapter 13: Contracts...169

Chapter 14: Horse Departure...176

Chapter 15: Final Words from Dante..183

Finding Dante...185

About The Authors...187

Resources 189

Acknowledgements...191

Preface

This book documents a conversation between myself, Cathy Seabrook, D.V.M. and Professional Animal Communicator, and my horse, Dante. Dante was a rescue horse who came with powerful teachings regarding general life and Horsedom. My initiation into animal communication came as a result of his severe lung disease. Only dire straits can convince veterinarians, so grounded in traditional veterinary medicine, to explore something as fantastically unbelievable as animal communication. Although veterinarians wish they could hear animals' thoughts, few actually believe in the reality of such an unscientific process.

Dante had small airway disease, similar to asthma in humans, triggered by an allergy to dust, molds and certain weeds in hay. He suffered from pneumonia when I found him which further damaged his respiratory system. He could not stop coughing from fall to spring and had no stamina or capacity for training or riding. I tried every medical cure known to veterinary medicine, various experimental cures, and recommendations from the Ontario Veterinary College. Nothing brought him relief and he was in serious trouble.

When I attended a training clinic in 2005, I met a sensible woman who happened to tell me of her unusual healing experience with a psychic healer. Having been initiated in that unconventional healing experience, she thought nothing would be lost if she dared to try animal communication when she had training issues with her horse, and got astonishing results in this field as well. At this point of veterinary helplessness I was ready to try anything to help my beloved horse, so I asked the woman without hesitation – "Do you think they know what medicine they need?" To which she replied, "There's only one way to find out."

And thus began my adventure into animal communication. I studied every means available to me in textbooks, DVDs, CDs and on the internet to educate myself and establish a basis of expectation to formulate questions to Dante.

Finally, after weeks of deciding on the proper questions, knowing this one chance would prove or disprove the entire theory for me, I sent my ten questions to the same animal communicator the woman had used in Connecticut, and told my horse in the pasture that someone was coming to talk to him on the airwaves. Dante paid no attention, so I told him twice, and then waited.

It seemed like forever but at last the letter arrived with the answers to my questions. I was more excited about this letter than my acceptance into Veterinary College! And it was awe inspiring. She described Dante perfectly with his explosive, unpredictable, dangerous emotions and recorded meticulously his delightful and insightful ideas on treatment and training. The definitive verdict was delivered in the results of a body scan that was included in the process (I had to ask her what that was when she offered it), and within that the communicator had noticed his right shoulder was higher than his left and that his right molars needed balancing. The body scan turned out to be correct, as he had a club foot due to injury before I found him, and the state of his molars was verified by the equine dentist shortly afterwards when she found extensive abnormalities demonstrated as wave mouth, cheek ulcers and slanted incisors, all on the right side of his mouth.

When the anatomical and medical evidence matched the body scan I could not deny there was something legitimate about animal communication. As much as I knew about animals after 24 years of veterinary practice, my whole perception of them had changed in that one letter from my horse!

Now how to learn it?! It was impossible at first. I tried every book and program I could find, and practised day in and day out, but I could not hear words from the animals. I began to understand their wishes more clearly, however, and due to my new perception changed how I practised veterinary medicine. I openly informed all my patients of the procedures within their clinical experience, including asking for compliance and forgiveness. My staff noticed the change in patient co-operation and also began explaining to the animals what was needed for ease in their clinical process.

But try as I might no words came clearly to me yet! So when a course was offered in England with Amelia Kincade, a famous Animal Communicator and Author, I signed up to be taught in person and participated in a class of over 80 students. And there I discovered I was somehow getting their messages because my answers were correct at the end of the class. At last communication had begun, but I needed to be able to verify it myself to believe in my abilities. I discovered a program called Animal Spirit Network in Illinois which ran a five level program, and I enrolled and completed that in two and a half years. It served to awaken animal communication skills powerfully for me, and hearing roared to the forefront along with other abilities I did not know existed within the experience, or life itself!

And then the animals began talking in all seriousness to me. Dante said he had a children's story to tell and so we created *Heart Hole Piece Named Horse*. And PETS said there had to be a book to help people address grieving and *Survive Saying Goodbye to Your Pet* was created, and then PUPPIES said they wanted a book (*Puppy Stuff by Puppies*), and likewise KITTIES (*Kitty Stuff by Kitties*) and PONIES (*Pony Stuff by Ponies*), and then HORSES wrote *Train Your Horses by Horses*.

And Dante told me he had another book, a very serious book, and so this book was born to explain the inherent power of spiritual horse, and it astounded me in the findings here, as we expect it will you as the reader. My entire perception of disease has shifted into another realm with the understanding attained in this conversation.

Embrace with me here the depth and grace that is Horse. Prepare to be charmed and educated about the benevolence in the gift of emotional release inherent in this magnificent creature, so willingly partnered with us in the energetic dance of all time. It is with gratitude and profound privilege that I present this private conversation for the growth of all who attract it to them.

It is intended to be read slowly, as some of the material is very deep. It is written exactly as told to me in horse prose, and although grammar is not essential to Horsekind, I have added it for ease of reading while preserving the original delivery. Enjoy your adventure into the explanation of the spiritual horse, by a horse. And never fear, for horses have many secrets left so as not to spoil the magic!

Forward

I feel like the most privileged horse person on the planet, doing this with you.

It is I, privileged horse, being with you at this right time.

How do you explain animal communication?

It is the synchronicity of two like-minded souls, engaging in an energetic flow of dialect that is only possible due to their similarity of consciousness and heart.

Few match up this way and so it is quite rare indeed to have the use of so many words in language, from animal to human.

We came for this of course, and our lives' paths matched more exactly than others with a similar talent for hearing from the animals.

It is all about wanting to hear so badly, that your request supersedes all else before you.

You asked your whole life to hear us; whether it was about fun, or illness, you said, "Tell me what to do!"

You added such emotion and heart to your request, and this is the result of that depth of asking.

I never really thought about writing a question and answer book with animal communication. Are there many horses that can do what we are doing here?

Not many.

More as the years go on, but there has not been such a connection as we have, with horse and vet animal communicator.

We planned this you know, and now we are living it.

How does a horse know so much about so many things?

I am a very old being.

Been around many centuries interacting with Mankind.

This base of dense involvement qualified me to tell you all of this.

I have endured much, learned more than most, and provided assistance for countless years to many.

That makes me qualified, so you know.

Tell me about knowing our stories.

Many of us have solid contracts with particular people.

We know what you endure to meet us to honour these contracts.

There is no choice in the honouring; they simply will be honoured.

So we have some idea always of your life and what brought us together.

We know things outside our horse circles because of our God-link and purpose with you.

It helps us decide on the best course of action and the timing of our work with you.

We appreciate your stories for you at times when you cannot, embrace all the energy you bring, and go from there to effect the highest good we can in your lives.

How much of our story did you know about?

All of it.

I knew your story of endurance too.

We are such a match you know.

I am relieved to say the troublesome teaching is over.

Tell me about endurance's purpose.

It builds the future fulfillment of powerful dream intention.

Without the endurance, the asking would be limited, small, and unexciting to spirit.

In the enduring of circumstance, and we by no means belittle circumstance, which may challenge you in your gut of guts, you ask beyond the opposite of the thing that troubles you so mightily.

And spirit answers in the beyond of the opposite of the endured.

We do not endure empty of necessity; it is built into our contracts with time and space.

See it as the empowering of you to be the brilliance you are, and were as you pondered what you deemed worthy to accomplish this lifetime.

You are the magnificence because of your enduring.

See it as teacher, see it as companion, and see it as gasoline for the trip to King and Queen you.

And yes, see it as lightly as possible even if it is difficult.

We can see it in a lighter framework for you, and you will often see horse in every attempt to uplift you to help you forget for one moment's worth your enduring.

It is not without great, great purpose in you.

Chapter One
Normal Life in Horsedom

What words do you have for me as we begin?

This will be really easy. Just follow my lead.

Tell me about being born.

It is a unique experience - a feeling of rushing forward into vast greatness, limitless expansion and accomplishment.

Mother is key to fulfilling intention and prophecy.

Not all of us get great mothers, but most of us get good mothers.

Mares know their key place in Horsekind and are revered in eternity for being mares.

Tell me about departing.

That's a different story now.

We choose when we have had enough of earth play.

We go in a variety of ways, and are quite indifferent to it in fact.

There comes a time when the physical magnificence pales, and the glory awaiting our transformation back to pure spirit is such a draw that we can no longer wait for the freedom we are remembering.

We meld seamlessly into pure spirit, ignoring the bodily agonies and last breaths, already galloping through Heaven's plains in glory unimagined by Mankind.

Nothing equals the experience of re-emerging with the fullness of God.

Tell me about age.

Age is a relative term, as spirit is ageless.

Only the body and mind reflect perceivable age.

We do not consider age at all really, once we have matured to adult physical horse.

Time simply goes on and on, year after year, as we work to our purpose.

If we thought of time as a boundary we could not think as clearly in our work with you.

Pressure to achieve would make us hurry, and our work cannot be hurried.

Old horses know so much and are a benefit to every horse herd, large and small.

Inherent knowledge is passed to younger horses and always powerfully aids their journey.

What's it feel like to gallop?

Imagine unrivaled power and speed, sight for miles and excitement of spirit directed by an all-seeing mind and limitless heart.

Imagine being one with the wind, sky and earth, and feeling their excitement compounding yours with every hoof strike.

Imagine every hoof strike delivering the energy of creation back to the earth, and every blade of grass celebrating the gift.

There is your beginning feeling.

Tell me about horse joy.

You have all seen it as we kick up our heels in appreciation for such exquisite physical make-up, combined with nature's gift of Day and all that brings in perception by our senses.

We see in such detail, hear from distant pastures, smell from winds that came twenty miles or more to give us their offering, and feel the combined Being of earth and sky, and all God melded together to create that moment.

Exploding bliss; nothing better.

Tell me about sadness and horse.

Yes, we know about sadness.

But it does not interfere with our ability to see the bigger picture.

We can be so practical for you about sadness, because it is but a blip in the story we know of you.

It may seem we are not sympathetic, but we love you too much to make a big thing about it at the time.

Trust we hear, sense, see and feel it from you - so there is no doubt.

But we are takers of difficult emotions and you can't make us cry in the taking.

We are above that to do what we do for you.

As for us, weep not for us in what appears to be difficult for us, for we come with a capacity to endure the physical, emotional, and mental aspects with a spirit strength surpassing your mind's ability to reason it.

This is horse at its fullest, seeing it but not being it, and transmuting it for the purpose of changing it back to good somewhere, sometime.

Yes, you've been sad, but that was then.

Tell me about mischief.

Such sheer delight exists in the mischievous horse.

We are, after all, so brilliant at it, and perceive every appreciation of our being from you, be it for entertainment value, beauty, or powerful achievement in our workplace.

Mischief has its own rewards because the energetic power in the thing we call smile rings in our very ears for hours afterwards.

It is such a simple thing, a smile, but the power it holds is not in imagination, for it really moves energy forward and into its space, touching everything in that precious deliverance.

Horse does not smile as you know it, but we are inducers of smile, which is our greatest glee.

Tell me about green grass.

We live for it and wait for it all winter here.

There is nothing like it for succulent feel and taste in our mouths.

God was sure thinking when he invented our synergy with grass.

Think about its position with the earth, how it grows without you making it grow, and think of its glory in its colour and symbology.

It represents eternal renewal of earth resource for all creatures, and we, horse, are able to sustain ourselves on this one innocent, only positive aspect of nature, when other creatures mostly eat other creatures.

Surely you see it could only be this way, existing without harm to the earth, for horse.

Tell me about fresh hay.

Ah - the anticipation we feel when the smell of hay is in the air.

A guarantee of good food always assures us.

We are like a child in a candy store about good food and enjoy it as much as you do.

Extras are so appreciated, always.

It is a gift to us, the food you bring, and we always send our appreciation whether you notice or not.

Do you know what plants are best not eaten?

We have a general idea depending on our upbringing and time with Mother.

Not all of us get sufficiently educated about food.

See how your children eat in spite of your knowledge about nutrition. Ours are the same.

Favorite colour of salt?

Yes, it's white.

Favorite colour?

Green, of course!

Tell me about water.

Cool, clear water is lifeblood to horse.

Many areas lack sufficient cleanliness.

We don't do well on murky water and its negative energy.

Water holds much symbolism for Mankind, representing life itself, and the cleansing action of water is active on many levels.

It is a carrier of stories, literally, in Nature, and benefits in the purposeful use to remove the energy in the dirt of the day, so to speak.

Should one encounter what they deem negative energy in their day, see the act of using water for its true use, carrying what is not beneficial back to positive energy.

It is read as a story to us as we see it in our environments, and felt as a purging and renewal as raindrops.

It is the same for Mankind really, but often it is not known all that water is to man.

Trust that the mere washing of hands removes energies that are stuck a bit in and on the physical man.

And yes, we enjoy for the most part the baths you give us, but temper the spray for us, knowing our sensitivity to touch outrivals all other creatures.

Tickle to horse is unperceivable to man.

Like a back slap to a bug, expect profound differences in perception here.

I love that example! Comment on bugs?

My personal detest.

There is nothing a bug is good for in my opinion.

Help us with this with every thought you can find.

The sprays are tolerable once we know your intention.

Banish them by all means possible.

And the horsefly?

See this as the Panzer tank of insects.

How did it get so resistant to spray and gentle thought?

It is deaf to pleas for co-operative dance with us, and the plague of Horsekind everywhere.

Shade is our only saving grace here, so make sure we have it to deal with this monster biter.

Tell me about grain.

This is one thing we appreciate more than most.

A regular feeding of grain says many things to us.

One, that you care enough to attend daily, and two, that our bodies are appreciated by you and you are striving to keep us fit and healthy.

Many horses require more grain than they are allotted.

Man doesn't always know our true requirements and energy expenditures.

We do appreciate all efforts to supplement our energy.

Tell me about treats.

Man can do no wrong with treats.

Horse looks forward to treats so much so that it is all we can think about in some situations.

Make us be polite and you have a perfect dance.

Tell me about sugar.

I love sugar as you know.

What could be better than sugar?

Does it rot your teeth?

Never.

Insufficient amount to affect our teeth.

Tell me about sleeping on your side.

Our moment when we submit to quiet of mind and body.

Soaking up the sun flat out is equal to spa time for human.

Nature is our masseuse, the earth is our welcoming bed, the wind is the caresse that rubs the sunshine oil into our coats, and the heartbeat of earth is clearly felt as ours touches it in that time of refreshing gift to horse from Earth.

Often many horses will sleep at the same time.

Yes, we know a good story is best shared.

So we sleep together, and know together the replenishment of side sleep.

Then we talk about the goodness of it in mutual benefit.

How does horse feel about living alone?

Not our ideal.

But we are adaptable and often accept the most un-horse-like situations for our relationship with you.

All things are endured with and for the right person.

There are no worries here; we can speak across the ages if we need too.

Why do horses pee in a freshly made up stall?

We are claiming our space.

It's a ritual of sacred proportions.

Just accept it as such and honour the behavior as powerful in spirit too.

What about marking territory with manure?

Yes, we all do that, but the stallion is the prominent marker.

And he insists on the honouring of his marksmanship.

Horses know about the honouring, but some people are ignorant of placement of manure significance.

Do not mess with a stallion's placement that delineates his ownership.

It could, and has, been deadly in history.

Can horses be asked to eliminate in certain places to keep main areas clean?

Yes, but we don't think that's important, so we keep forgetting you asked.

We don't mind manure in general places.

Tell me about eating manure.

There's a story in every manure pile, of course.

We read the story, and sometimes it is so good we take a nibble or two for greater participation in it.

Why do you chew trees?

They have something precious to give horse in bark and story.

All we eat has a story for us, and we love a good story.

So see us eating the magnificent tree and taking in a piece of its magnificence, and weep not for tree as it is generous of nature and heart to all beasts and birds.

It would not come as tree if this were not so, it would come as rock.

Why is it so fun to break out of your field?

We seek adventure in the distant places where wind comes from and the stories live.

Don't you strive to know of new experiences paired with Dream and Promise?

So is the nature of horse driven to bust through the fence and run toward Promise.

And once we taste of Promise in the nearby field or down the road, we always want to see more.

So your breachy horses, as you call them, are just the most adventurous in spirit.

Tell me why you stand in the rain when the barn door is open.

There is nothing like the washing-of-tears-away feeling in rain.

We don't cry, but such a cleansing occurs in the pelting of raindrops, grounding us to earth and replenishing our spirit journey with you.

You feel it too, those of you who run in the rain barefoot, mindless in your delight.

All is new and fresh after standing in the rain.

And thunderstorms?

Different story.

We prefer not to be pelted to bits, and we will use the barn door as a rule if it is available.

Still cleansed and grounded, as rain is rain.

Tell me about the sun, the moon and the stars and horse.

We are all dance partners with you.

All things are part of these.

It is so pure a connection that mourning occurs deprived of sun, moon and stars.

Self from self, as one talented man called it.

See horse as the star itself, and you will more clearly understand the distance when horse rarely sees the stars at night.

Horses left inside miss stars in the way people miss people they love.

Distant relatives always are appreciated – and yes, we get the joke!

Tell me about scratching your friends with your teeth.

It is an acknowledging of acceptance of full horse before us.

We will not do this with everyone, as you know.

But the horses we share this behavior with are bonded for life in all aspects, as long as they may be physically kept together.

It represents a deep association between horses.

Not for just any old horse.

And swishing tails for each other?

Co-operation and energy efficiency.

Why not share my precision aim with my tail?

If I get the end of horse tail in my face, what was that about?

You were graced more than anything.

We just shared as if you were horse.

What's that about when horses bite other horses?

You trespassed into my space to deserve a bite correction.

I warned you first.

Never think you weren't warned most graciously.

What about a kick?

Nervy little rip to have to raise up to a kick.

I had to up the ante here.

And a strike?

The horse who offers strike is struggling with the emotion-mental-biology thing in horse, and was rushed into comprehension which was not available to him.

He had to say, wait don't trespass here, I have not made sense of it, not deemed it worthy, not deemed you worthy to present this thing that I can't yet think about.

Do not come any closer!

Tell me about the speed of deliverance.

You won't see it if you blink.

We strike with speed of spirit because it is a spirit striven struggle to come to grips with the thing before us.

Not all horses strike, but those of us who feel extreme protection is required to preserve sanity in the situation will strike with pre-eminent precision and skill unmatched in Mankind's boxing derivative.

What are the warning signs of these three?

For a bite, I already looked at you with daggers, then I moved my head and ears, then I moved my neck and shoulders, and then I moved my teeth.

Lots of time there to change your mind and behave yourself.

I speak as if you are the colt I have been enlisted to teach.

If I go to kick, I have done all of this and added a tail flick gesture which is your last warning.

If I strike, you won't have much time to see it coming.

I will choose strike only if the situation is so extreme that warning is as pointless as co-operation is in the moment.

Is there such a thing as a love bite?

You tell me.

Not in my thinking.

I might nip but it was intentional if I just brushed you with my teeth.

Nips are how we say it louder than posture, and like a whisper it is used only on loved ones.

Tell me about licking and chewing.

Best said as, "Whew. Got through that, thankfully. Now what?"

What about licking our hands?

You taste of good things if you have handled food for us.

We seek the molecules left there.

What kind of affection do you appreciate from us?

We like food-attention-affection and we like stroking if it is not on our faces.

If you must rub faces do it on our big old foreheads and not on our noses.

Many of us tolerate hugs as we understand the meaning of it for you, but we need a relationship with you to begin to tolerate the squeezing pressure of a hug.

Saddles hug, but many of us lack full appreciation of it.

So see it for temporary squeeze value and restraint, before see it as affection.

But we get it for you and accept it for what it is in its deepest offering as love for us.

We tolerate thumps by hand as it means something to you, but it is a clamouring of sensation to us in its pat-pat-pat.

We do not dwell on the presentation of affection, endure all forms that disguise as affection, and know it comes from the deepest best place no matter how it feels to us.

This affection can be expressed in quiet standing together with us as easily, or sitting in solitude with us, as we read heart, thought and feeling from you regardless of touch from you.

Affection is in a look, a care duty to us, a thought to do something for us, care for our environment, suitable comfortable tack, how you use the reins, how you sit on us, and how you ask us to do anything with you.

It is in all of our interactions, and we read every moment's gift with constant recognition and appreciation.

Not so touchy feely then.

Not at all.

It is the energy behind the doing that you know as affection that we read.

Lots of us kiss you.

Yes.

And some of us kiss you back.

If you have a kissing horse he has come with an affection contract of special degree.

Tell me about me hugging you.

I got used to it frankly.

Now I actually enjoy it for the most part, now that our hearts are so similarly healed.

I love you Dante.

And you know I love you back, beyond language.

Chapter Two

Different Kinds of Horse

Tell me about your personalities.

That's a big topic.

We are not one alike.

There are silly horses, practical horses, reverent horses, teacher horses, follower horses, pregnant horses, thoughtful horses, violent horses, war horses, peace horses, seeker (lost) horses, find and keeper horses, stick-to-it horses, sickly horses, tough horses, soft horses, puppy dog horses, work-a-holic horses, long suffering horses, game playing horses, serious horses, and spirit guide horses.

Not all of us laugh.

Do you talk differently?

Oh yes.

Some of us have a lot to say, and some of us prefer more silence.

We have learned to speak through motion, and posture.

Not so many have the opportunity to speak with words, but we all are capable of it.

We don't grieve missing the opportunity to use words, but revel when it comes.

Every word is weighed and counted before used.

It may be our only opportunity to be heard, you understand.

I am an exception, and thrilled to have the chance to speak my mind, which is a very big one.

There is no mistake in this pairing.

It was set long ago and the story is wondrously entertaining.

You should tell them at some point how you found me, and how I waited for you.

I will do that.

Tell me about the violent horses. I was surprised to see this as horse character.

Some of us can't tolerate negative energy violation.

It so goes against our view of our particular purpose that lifetime and we rebel.

It's that simple.

We know it will shorten our duration of bombardment.

Horses that are violent got so lost in the negativity, be it abuse or neglect, or blindness in Mankind to certain situations with no hope in sight for repair or change, that they go mad with hopelessness.

Hopelessness in beings grounded in hope so goes against our inherent nature; insanity is the only option.

The lost horses?

Some never find their purpose satisfying, because they aimed too low.

They wander until they get another chance, and know more the next time.

Find and keeper horses?

You and me.

Contract bound before our time together.

Many horses choose this category, and of course we get to choose.

Pregnant horses?

Some are only mothers.

They accept it with little say in the matter.

Few choose it again, given the chance.

Motherhood is wonderful, but does not fulfill complete purpose.

It is not rewarding because of the early separation of mother and foal in many cases.

Many search for understanding in this realm.

Not enough preparation is provided for the mothers or the foals to be parted, when it is all they know as life.

Stick-to-it horses?

These give their all no matter what.

They never rebel, never object, offer compliance in the field, and often excellence in performance.

Duty bound horses.

Soldiers drilled into obedience, regardless of circumstance.

Game-playing horses?

Everyone knows when they have one of these.

Constant entertainment, toddler-like, you can't take your eyes off them or they have committed mischief.

Reverent horses?

These horses endure with us.

Suffering is part of their initiation.

It empowers them to heal on a deeper level, so see them in therapy situations.

Silly horses?

These horses are light-hearted to the degree that nothing bothers them or is of significant detriment to them.

They see nothing to forgive, blessed with the inability to recognize mistakes in others.

Given the opportunity in an unsuitable environment they will simply opt out early to re-try somewhere else.

Smiling is part of their daily expression and they use interesting phrases like "no big whoop".

You see why I call them silly.

Serious horses?

These come with powerful purpose.

There is no distraction from it, and life involves little play.

They seem to come alive in competition and real work, and many are in industries like logging in this day and age.

Loving, giving, industrious horses.

They live to wear harness, literally.

Follower horses ?

These horses seem unable to function without a clear leader.

They lack ability to maintain a long focus, and only feel confident behind a leader.

You find many of these in wrangler outfits as trail horses, or riding stable horses.

They are content in the simple life, still able to be of benefit to Mankind, while following.

Many introduce people to the wonders of horseback riding in a safe environment.

Horsekind has deep, deep appreciation for this horse, revering their peaceful role in introduction.

Thoughtful horses?

Many is the time man has stood deep in thought admiring the peace presence surrounding the free horse.

These horses provoke thought in Mankind.

Thoughts are not limited to peace; thoughts about glory, riches, respect, freedom and God are evoked from horse.

Some horses are better at evoking than others.

Work-a-holic horses?

These poor devotees came to work.

They are the beasts of burden in Horsedom, and we all recognize them when we see them.

Ribs are an obvious feature, with sad eyes in a downcast frame of reference.

They choose difficult situations, and difficult hearts to remodel, and endure not without hope.

Weeping for them is what changes hearts the fastest.

These horses endure because they know time is waiting for no man.

Practical horses?

We all want one of these fellows.

Happy at any occupation, easy to train for common purpose, and happy-go-lucky for the most part.

Most of these are geldings, obviously.

Teacher horses?

Brilliant minded beings with great intelligence.

These horses choose placement in particular environments and come with great contracts individualized prior to arrival here.

No mistake in the pairing with this kind of horse, and the human will have endured much to deserve the combination of man and horse.

With this type of being, huge leaps forward are always possible.

This type of horse will challenge the individual profoundly to enact necessary change for life situations the human must face.

And yes, there are many combinations possible in the teaching realm of Horsedom.

War horses?

Think how Mankind has used this particular horse.

Powerful in mind, body and soul to uphold Mankind in something he believes in but the horse does not.

What grace has governed this type of horse over time man cannot comprehend.

Still man uses Horsekind for this purpose, and still horses come forward of such fortitude recognized in superior officers in the armed forces.

Bravery in the face of certain physical demise, while holding spirit firmly unshakeable.

We bow to this horse.

Peace horses?

The keepers-of-kindness is how you see them.

Often in surprising places - a buggy in a city, a pony in a yard; these remind you of gentler times, and happy days, and childhood dreams.

The feeling you get when you see or stumble on these horses is where they get their name.

A reminder in a busy day to bring you back to where your heart needs to be.

Sickly horses?

We are not all born to be magnificent, but we are born to change lives.

Sometimes an illness or deformity plants softness in a heart that grows from there, and once the seed is planted the job is done.

These horses know the change they effect.

Do not weep for them for they are among the most powerful life-changers in Horsedom.

Tough horses?

These horses see all, endure all, know all and forgive all.

They live long lives to be so wise.

Tough skin is the mask they wear to negate wrong doing for not just themselves, but Mankind.

They hold man in a sacred space of benevolence unmatched.

Few feel it, but many wonder what it is about a particular horse that makes all else bearable.

These are the bishops in our society.

Prayer, if horse felt that necessary, would be their language.

Soft horses?

These little guys win hearts by their cutie-pie looks and mannerisms.

Without them horse world would not be complete in that it could not reach those un-athletic enough to ride or drive.

These horses you can hold in your lap.

Many choose this option today, as it is so sweet and easy to win hearts by being cute.

Puppy-dog horses?

Catchy phrase for those horses so easy going in nature anyone can do anything with them.

Their compliance makes them so loveable and they win many hearts worldwide.

They prefer not to compete, and are better off that way.

Long-suffering horses?

This type of horse endures with high purpose.

Only enduring suffering creates powerful, powerful relationships with like-minded, like-matched people.

There is a drawing of these horses to their people in accordance with strict contractual timing.

While some horses do not choose to remember their trials, these horses remember every detail, with the capacity to forgive and knowledge of the building blocks the challenges represented on their journey to their matched soul-person.

Spirit guide horses?

Yes. At last we come to this.

There are those beings so entrenched in spirit duty, shall we say, that every minute detail of their lives is dedicated and devoted to the completion and maturation of soul necessary to belong to an individual where the earth rules are broken, literally, to accommodate spiritual growth in the person.

How does a horse accomplish what a person thinks they accomplish?

The horse *be-s* the thing that shakes the ground under the person's feet, shakes their take on the world, and shakes their lives into betterness.

This sacred contract has no limitations.

These pairs, horse and person, are the ones who make masterpieces of life in healing on all levels of physical, mental, emotional and spiritual.

The combination is a synergy, growing beyond expected proportion and is limitless in God's eyes.

Many, many horses are here, now, at this contractual level, changing lives, noticed and unnoticed.

People look back and see what their horse did for them and the grace and awe is apparent in the backward look.

The journey itself may not be that much fun, but the end result is always worth it.

And you?

I am a most excellent combination of spirit guide, teacher, serious and magic counsellor, created especially for our contract to enable you to meet your other contracts of obligation and exquisite, delightful dessert.

Thank-you so much Dante.

Unnecessary, but appreciated nevertheless.

Chapter Three
Horse Families

Let's talk about horse families.

Let's do that.

Mother and Father – how do you describe your relationship with them?

We are much alike in our feelings for parents.

Father horse is fairly indifferent to us, knowing his part in our process is brief.

Mother is the opposite, demonstrating all capacity for love as many humans know it.

Mother is a Universal term in many species, as you can recognize when you see it.

Mother imparts integrity of purpose, respectful communication, and rules and regulations of Horsedom, like stay by me when my head is up, and do what you like when I am eating.

Mother teaches touch is good.

Mother gives her life for foal, and calls long after he has moved on.

This call rocks the horse world, as we all hear you have gone from Mother.

Some mothers, especially those whose foals are not ready for purpose, withhold all adventure into affection as the loss would be too unforgivable for such heart driven beings.

So some are spared.

You have seen some mothers indifferent as sires when the foal has died.

They were held in a precious place of knowing, seeing the foal in new fulfilled life elsewhere.

That is all they can see at that time, as it must be softened somehow.

Tell me about mares.

Mares.

Who can resist a good mare?

The best mares seem to be used as mothers, but that is not always their calling.

Mares are teachers of high degree and very specific in that.

Precision is a mare's quality.

Respect is expected for mares, and fillies learn this at a very young age.

Little tolerance is given for disrespectful behavior.

I personally always watch my Ps and Qs around all mares; it's just right.

Tell me about stallions.

It's a lonely life being a stallion.

Few would choose it if given a choice.

We are a misunderstood group as stallions, and unable to demonstrate with finesse and gentlemanly behavior our true nature, for the most part.

It takes an exceptional person to understand a stallion with clarity.

Sometimes stallions lack the best equine instruction as a youngster, and this makes for a poorly behaved adult.

No horse likes to see his life not reach its potential.

Stallions deserve great praise for their accomplishments, which are achieved amidst indescribable distraction.

Tell me about foals.

Yes.

Such delightful packages full of wonder and play, and accidental learning.

Legs all over the place.

It is a necessary part of being a horse, but many foals are removed from their dam before they have their questions asked.

This is the only bad part about being a foal.

Tell me about geldings.

Now we come to the most generous natured sex.

For steady and reliable use a gelding has no match.

It is unfortunate that many of us would make excellent sires, but there are already many unwanted horses per se, in the world.

Gelding us is a necessity and we accept it fully and embrace the consequences of unchallenged relationships with people.

Tell me about eohippus.

Long ago we were very small, in dream state it seems.

We dreamed about our future in detail and suffice it to say, we achieved our dreams.

Let no man ever despair at dreams - look what we achieved!

Tell me about the wild horse herd.

This particular kind of horse remains unspoiled on purpose.

There is a huge statement about freedom here, but paired with an acceptance of pairing with Mankind if possible.

We are reminded of days when thought and movement was unrestricted, and we dared think about God full-time-ish.

Now we have many things to think about, but God is always at our core of being, smiling at us.

Who is the herd boss really?

Of course the mare is.

Who else?

In a society where motherhood directs the future of the outcome of purpose, a strong persistent voice must lead.

Mare never gives up on directing.

Mare never tires of answering her children's questions.

Geldings and stallions have little interest in children, and while we agree to assist in their education, it is Mare who oversees and guards their intellect, manners and dreams.

Who picks the leader?

We get to choose the most suitable leader, by acknowledging physically her stature.

It is no mistake that the most boisterous characteristics win this position.

But we accede to this process with full acceptance and recognition of the rightful place of that prominent, bossy, beautiful being.

What exactly does the stallion do?

Well, he thinks he is the leader, as this kind of thinking is necessary for a stallion.

He creates the commotion that gets us moving when we have to move.

He keeps order amongst the rowdy youngsters and makes them strive to be stronger.

He demonstrates courage more than most expect of a horse, and his superior dedication to his human is often marvelled at.

If you get a really good stallion, you have the best of horse world.

However, the match in Mankind must also be exceptional.

Too many unsuitable mismatches and they are very, very dangerous.

The stallion demands your full attention, and accepts nothing less.

Rarely is there an exception to this rule.

The youngsters – tell me about their education.

They must learn to run from danger, that's number one.

Stick to mother like they are one, no matter what, unless she is eating or sleeping, that's the rule.

Mother is driven to these first rules.

Then they must be respectful.

This occupies nearly all of the mare's time, and is often exhausting to the point that the odd time, baby strays.

In the wild this can be fatal, so mares in the wild seem to never sleep.

They simply must be more attentive.

Mares in captivity have lots of help, it seems, raising baby, but raise baby they must, or the end result is troublesome.

Never let a foal raise itself, or a group of foals raise themselves.

Mares must be allowed to educate the foals, and foals must get to ask their questions.

Early weaning deprives foals of asking, and this creates confusion for many, many horses.

It's like never learning to read and now your life depends on knowing the words in the book.

Do you get to decide if you come as a wild horse?

Of course there is some major input whether to come domesticated or wild.

Most of us can fulfill larger purpose domesticated, so this is generally chosen.

Horses that want a bit of a break may choose to come as wild horses.

Have you ever been part of a wild herd?

Never.

I always interacted with man intimately.

Does Mother tell you about man?

Oh yes, many stories.

Especially the good ones.

Some mothers have not had the greatest experiences with man, but they are wise enough to spare babies those tales.

If mother has never known kindness from man, baby will only know that.

Does Father have an opinion about being called indifferent?

Of course not, it is his nature and he is quite proud of it.

What about brothers and sisters?

We know of them but have a different type of relationship with them, being fairly independent of siblings.

Aunts and Uncles, Grammas and Grampas?

We have those aunts that help care for babies, related or not.

Grandmother horses rarely get to be with their grand-foals, but when that combination is possible nothing is impossible for the foal.

Now he receives knowledge of the generations of Horsekind, and that bond is tight indeed.

You have witnessed this, where grandmother stayed in body when foal needed her.

The pull is strong in this bond to support, especially if Mother is gone.

All elderly horses are priceless teachers for foals and older youngsters, but many lack sufficient patience for their shenigans.

What about horse best friends?

This plays a very significant role in horse life.

We all adore someone.

It could be either sex as best friend, but we are often sweet on mares as geldings.

They are not always so sweet back.

There was a movie where horse best friends were portrayed, and one horse protected the other when he was weak. Is there reality here?

Not so much, we are often alone in our situation.

But it does not mean we are not loyal as friends.

If there were some way to demonstrate friendship in a situation we might, or we might not bother.

The horse friend knows the love bond is unshakeable regardless.

We are not petty about any of this, knowing the depth of bond is deep beyond words.

What about lovers?

You make me smile.

Of course, we have deep love with certain horses.

This creates an eternal space for us, and we always attempt to return in some manner together.

It is eternal as you think it is, love a horse has for another horse.

When a horse you love dies and departs from physical, we often see demonstrations that look like you are weeping or missing the one that has departed.

Of course, we know they are gone, but the physical energetic field remains until it is stagnant.

So we stand around in the remnant of the physical, feeling the goodness of the relationship.

We are not grieving, for that would be against true nature of horse, but we like that you think us possible of that.

When the energetic remnant is wispy and has wafted into the spirit fully, we are no longer interested in looking "sad", as there is nothing left to interest us.

We know the being is pure, spiritual, glorious energy, which is what we will be one day too.

It is all a sacred wondrous dance of energies, and we either dance here in physical, or we dance there in spirit.

There is no grief, just enjoyment of those good feeling energies that were the Being, and are still the Being, of that horse.

Anytime we wish, we can communicate with those departed from physical, and anytime they can participate in a moment with us in physical.

So if there is a need to feel a full gallop, they are there with us in it.

When your person dies, or a person you just love anyway, how do you feel about that?

We are aware of the gap in space they left here with you and us.

It is just like the departed horse friend, or other animal friend.

There are lovely energies floating in the space that we take part in with you.

If only we could remind you there is just pure positive around that space.

We are partaking of the sweetness of energy that we experienced as you or our friend, here in this physical space, that was God where we came from, and God where we go to.

This sweet energy dilutes and dissipates, but while we are in the sweetness of your departure, we are reminded fully of our experience when we are directly before God.

So we relish it and remember.

People grieve.

Yes.

They do not fully understand the communication still available to them as we do, and feel the departure is a tearing apart instead of an edification of the sweetness of that being, now fully, directly, in full view of God.

I like to think I will be in Heaven with you and other horses I have loved when I depart.

There is always that option, truly.

Once you depart and have full view of all that was and is, and much of what will be, you will make a decision about what to sustain and what to just sleep with in spirit.

We will all be there of course to help you decide.

Reminders of our lives together will be part of the atmosphere eternally.

We have much to learn from horse Dante.

Isn't that the case?

Chapter Four

Foals

Do foals come in all different characters or do they develop the qualities of those characters on their journey?

They come ready for purpose, so character is already set in the biology form.

Every foal knows its inherent contracts, but they seem to sleep while babyhood is endured.

Do foals talk the same as adult horses?

There is no baby talk in Horsedom, but there are shorter sentences, so to speak.

For the most part, foals can converse with communicators immediately, as this is a spirit based language.

What kind of questions do foals ask their mothers?

Where's the milk?

This question preoccupies their thinking for some time, as they expand into their environment.

As soon as the foal is confident about knowing this answer, he is free to grow into more interesting questions.

What is the moon for Mother?

Why does the sun go down?

When is my person arriving?

Why are my legs so gangly?

What's that on my nose?

Where's the point in work?

Will I suffer on my studies?

Will I return to you someday?

Can we still talk later on?

Who is Father?

What is slaughter?

Will I endure until my person?

Will I have many persons?

Is it time for lunch now?

And so on…

Imagine all the questions you could ask if you had speech at birth.

Imagine having the purest knowing of good in all things, and asking from a Sweetness and a Forgiving Place.

All foals are born with speech capability, and all they need is time to ask the questions of Mother.

This is their true asking of Mankind, let me be with Mother long enough.

Tell me how to raise a foal.

Teach us manners gently.

We are just so curious and expecting good things of you.

Don't let us be raised without a parent of some sort.

We run amuck left to our own devices, and run into trouble later when no-one prepared us for interaction with people.

Saturate foals with loving experiences and fair play.

Do they have an age at which they would like to begin training?

They all wish to wait as long as possible.

Youngsters are youngsters after all.

Give them time to be as horse a little while - two years if possible.

Then begin some easy lessons on line.

They wish to be three before you sit on them the first time.

Not only is body mature enough, but mind and biology have a distinct advantage at three, because the time has allowed compounding of processes to learn so much faster.

Purpose is foremost by three years of age in horse.

Waiting longer is wasting time for them.

Tell me how to start a colt.

Always with other horses present, saddled or free.

Pick the best baby-sitter available to steady our emotions for us.

Everything is challenged including our balance, which is very precious to us.

Be easy on our mouths, for our first opinion of the bit is made in the first exposure to it, and is hard to change later.

Use your best to start the babies, for they need it.

Always be kind first, and firm second.

We are trying to understand and being flooded with stimulation that requires response, and often we have no idea what that response should be.

Take it slow, if you can.

Give us many, many breaks.

The person who starts us gives us a lasting impression of all people in our lifetime.

We can forgive a bad colt start, but it is easier to prevent a problem than fix it, because our memories are great indeed.

Tell me what fillies think about most.

Will they respect me like Mother?

Every endeavor is made to mimic a powerful mother.

See fillies trying out bossiness at very early ages.

Let their bravado go for the most part, for the best mares are bossy, bossy mares.

What about colts?

Nothing enters a colt's mind other than dominance play.

Run faster, down on his knees, fight-fight-fight with all male horses.

Size has no command over impressing others.

It is the colt who bites and shoves that wins the horse play, and this has no reflection on his purposeful behavior.

The most boisterous colts make the most powerful characters.

Quiet little colts have meeker thoughts and smaller contracts with people.

Look to the rowdy colts for great teachers later on.

What is colt's opinion on age to be gelded?

Never.

Just kidding.

We prefer to be two, and informed of the procedure ahead of time if possible.

Explain why on earth you would do this to such an excellent specimen of horse, and we will try to accommodate the understanding of it.

What is the display about when foals do the grimace and champ their teeth?

It is about making a boo-boo.

They went too far and kai-yai like a crying baby.

We see it as apologizing for overstepping their bounds, and always accept the apology.

Tell me about foals that die young.

These foals lost their way to their purpose.

They choose to re-start again elsewhere.

Few return to the same situation or location.

They pick the easiest way to return to spirit and often baffle the caregivers.

It's all about the energetic environment and being able to manage the energy where they end up.

Sometimes the mare makes sure the baby is prepared better for awakening, but sometimes the mare knows it is for the best this time.

The foal does not feel bad, knowing it can come back anytime it wishes.

Did they get confused because they are so new?

Partly.

The way was not clear enough for them on all levels of physical, emotional, mental and spiritual.

Rather than go at purpose half-masted, they choose to return with more clarity, and always achieve it the next try.

I have had some experience with foals dying. The circumstances have dumbfounded the people concerned. Is that generally the situation?

It always seems a mystery as to how the baby could have injured itself so badly, or colic-ed, or faded.

When the mystery is noticed, you always know it was a spirit driven reason.

Still sad for the people, but necessary for the foal.

Why do foals get aborted?

As we talked about before, there can be a mix-up about purpose.

Sometimes the mares see this and decide for the foal.

This grieves them not because we are about spirit driven purpose.

It is no shame to start again, and we are not sentimental in our decisions not to come forward at that moment.

If people really understood our nature, they would grieve less at lost baby horses.

Tell me about orphan foals.

These little guys came with such independent spirit.

They are fully prepared for orphan-hood by Mother.

Don't weep for them, as they come with such strong opinions which will be sharpened by life and everyone they interact with.

Above all, don't let them abuse you!

Give them a good teacher horse that is very, very bossy - not the most tolerant horse available.

These horses grow to be powerful thinkers, but at least teach them Horsedom for their base.

Many orphans are exiled because man forgot to tell them they were horses.

There was mass abortion in the Thoroughbred industry several years ago. Tell me about that.

Those mares spoke as loudly as they could against principles they disagreed with.

Change needed to come regarding decisions man makes about breeding so many horses, with so many horses being discarded if they do not reach a level of monetary competence.

The mothers decided to rebel, so to speak, and this is how they did it.

People searched for a biological reason.

Yes, they found a tiny culprit to blame, because they could not accept a reason from another realm.

But it was a spiritual decision, as you know.

Deformities. Why do some horses have deformities?

Again, the foal has choice about staying or leaving.

A foal may try life out, so to speak, coming with bent limbs.

If he sees this lifetime has all the possibilities he hoped for, he can straighten around and stay.

If he needs convincing, he may tolerate corrective treatment until he is convinced.

But if he sees he will have great trouble succeeding in purpose, he will defy correction and go back to try again.

What about wry noses in foals?

These babies are making a huge statement.

They extract massive sympathy and it serves their temporary emergence.

Sometimes knowing the softness of Mankind's heart entices a re-entry as a more powerful aspect of horse, and this is one way to convince horse to aim higher next time if that had not been explored beforehand.

What's up with mares that reject their foals?

These mares never chose Motherhood.

It was forced on them.

They are not prepared in mind or body, and seem to disconnect from the entire situation long before the foal attempts to nurse.

Why are certain breeds demonstrating this more?

No particular reason.

This is a misnomer in reality.

Many mares object, some just object more obviously.

Dante and Cathy Seabrook, D.V.M.

Tell me about horse's impression of imprinting.

This can go one of two ways for horse.

Either the imprinter imparts a gentle touch that ensures the foal's love of people and early dedication to his purpose with them, or it establishes a lifelong hardness of surface in those that suffer harshness in the process.

We recognize fully the measure of imprinting touch done with love, or done with science of desensitization that rings on our nerves like chalk on a board noises, literally screeching us into an ability to ignore that which might otherwise inspire us.

There must be love in the touch to endear us to purpose with you, because such a fine line is walked at this time of our lives as to almost ruin our sensitive nature by drowning it out in self-preservation.

Go easy with this process you call imprinting, for it is our first association with you at a precious time of acclimatizing to the energy of earth versus Heaven, as you call it.

Do foals prefer ranch raising or home raising?

We all love freedom.

If we could be ranch raised we could dwell on Horse-ness longer and learn so much from the herd before launching into a career.

The difference between ranch youngsters and home raised youngsters is the degree of tolerance for boo-boos on Mankind's part.

The ranch colt cares not for mistakes in his start, but the home raised youngster has immense tolerance having been socialized since infancy with touch and noise, and the commotion of Mankind.

Ranch raised colts seem to go straight to purpose once started, having had such a lengthy pre-school in Horsedom to prepare them for true purpose.

Home raised babies like to wander aimlessly, delaying purpose until a later time, and suddenly man is seated on a 7 year old for the first time, who has no respect for real work, and finds it hard to connect with his purpose.

Many horses prefer home raising for the fact that they are less likely required to earn their keep, and get away with everything in their cuteness, and sometimes too much.

Find a balance in the home raised foals that teach them the value of horse work, as cute as they may seem.

We came for real work with you.

We appreciate that you think us cute, or beautiful, but give us real purpose as early as possible and our beings will thrive and prosper on every level with you.

What would foals like to tell people?

We would like to say be considerate of our explorations towards you.

We rarely think about consequences of actions when so young.

The world is just a magical place full of wonder as long as Mother is there to oversee our responses to things.

Don't let us have a bad experience with you, or the rope, or the trailer.

Prevent what you can, and soothe us through the rest of it.

We are gentleness at our base, with curiosity icing.

Help us believe in you early, and this will help us establish our purpose firmly early in our relationship.

Chapter Five

Performing as Horse

Tell me about purpose here with us.

We came for great relationships.

We came to show intelligence in form, thought and spirit.

We use our supreme gifts to help you endure what troubles come in earth playtime, seeing it as such.

There is no real trouble at the bottom of things.

We know this.

We hold you in a revered bubble of benevolence and love beyond love that you have insufficient language for.

We have the language known as Horse, such an all encompassing term for the magnificence that represents our kind.

We are movement and language and spirit held consciousness of such a degree it can't be described - but we try.

Tell me how you feel about regular horse work with us.

Yes, that.

All part of the base to take you deeper.

We had to entice you somehow.

Horse 101 you might say.

We accept it all and fly with it, recognizing it is the opening to your heart.

We see the door and lead you through it with regular horse work.

It is still fun for us as a rule - at least we try to see it that way for the most part.

Some of us have harder roles than others obviously.

Some of us choose not to last long if we see our life will not be effective in our situation.

Don't be sad for us with this, as we have great purpose in all aspects of our lives with you, and most of you begin to recognize that as your eyes open on our journey together.

It is really all good, and we accept what you ask of us as a general rule, especially when you ask with reverence in your heart.

Is some of the regular horse work monotonous?

Of course. We learn much faster than you do.

It's all about survival in a one-way situation.

People want us to do their idea long before they think we have ideas.

That's how it always was, man thinking he had the superior thinking.

Dante and Cathy Seabrook, D.V.M.

We go along with it because it suits our purpose of introduction - nothing more.

We could try sending messages in the beginning but they generally don't get heard, so we go along with things the best we can until our window of opportunity opens for communion with you.

Just how it works best in the general scheme of things.

We are most accepting of all good intentions, seeing clearly the end result of our union.

Some of us see past the present relationship to our future bond with who we intended to be with this lifetime, and simply hold that in our focus, knowing it comes and the present time is our moment of preparation for what lies ahead of us.

We are such accepting creatures, as we meant to be from the beginning.

Surely you see that now.

Tell me how you train to your purpose.

We come with an intention to serve as Emotional Healers and Spiritual Holders for you.

We come as proud physical beings capable of great athleticism, our "in" with you.

If all you knew us as was cuddle bunnies, we could not be as effective.

We came capable of warfare, which we knew Mankind would need, we came capable of speed and power, and we came capable of creating bonds of love that would shake Mankind into recognition of animals as spiritual beings.

And we came beautiful too.

This drew you in with our dark and wondrous eyes, shiny coats, prancing gait and flowing hair.

Beauty always helps in Horsedom.

We took that base foundation, and applied understanding and forgiveness to Mankind's exercises of life.

We gave our all, as recorded in your history books

What isn't often told is how big the "all" was.

Our inherent purpose isn't something trained, it is something *being* in us, Horse, so profound a part of our creation, that we forget to speak of it, or even remember it.

We just *are* the help you need, whatever shape or form that requires in the moment, in the year, and in the century.

Like the Fly in the birds, the gift in horse is in the being with you, where you are the better of you, the fullness of you and what you came to discover.

We are the helpers that uphold you in your most God-like version of you.

Sometimes you feel this so palpably.

You feel the wonder, and think it's us, but it's really this in you.

Let's talk about earth performance. Tell me about show horses.

Now we are getting somewhere.

This area of interest fascinates those meant to participate.

We revel in accomplishment with our people.

Most horses intended for this purpose have exceptional tolerance for minute demands of the show circuit.

Many others would not be so tolerant of picky points that are so unnatural to horses.

Many horses love the imagery and theatre in the show circuit, while for others it seems a fate worse than death, to quote a meaning people understand.

Tell me about jumping.

Not my thing obviously.

But those who come to jump can't help themselves.

It is so inherent in their choice they demonstrate their ability almost from day one.

To many horses it is comical how the jumping horse would bother to go over an obstacle almost higher than themselves, but to each his own.

Jumping is as close as we come to mimic flying, and is one way we hook a lot of people into horse ownership.

So it has its uses.

Tell me about racing.

Another form of flying - sophisticated flying.

This area of horse use has endured many good and bad reviews over thousands of years.

Revered as the elite of horses, the race horse suffers from misuse in its breeding program.

Too many hopefuls enter with odds that are hard to beat.

The ones who go down in history had contracts so big they could not fail.

Heart and soul has long belonged in the racing industry, of both horse and Mankind.

And yes, God came as a horse in Secretariat.

And we all watched and cheered as the unbelievable was witnessed and hearts grew the world over.

Tell me about pulling.

These horses come to work and revel in their power.

There's no kidding around in this department.

Seriously, this occupation demonstrates commitment in spades to representation of the horse's contribution to the past, to history, to never forgetting what horse has done for man's livelihood over the lifetime of the world.

Tell me about dressage.

See how horse has taken war and made it beautiful.

Every movement here was finessed from our war manoeuvres, be it the proud carriage of the general, or the dalliance with sword.

This elegant sport, of sorts, is not for every horse.

The demands on compliance with constriction are high, and radiance in spite of this must still come through.

Many horses in this field die younger than normal, having given so much in their shorter lifetimes.

It is a sad fact that can be stated without remorse, as these horses take pleasure in their high degree of education for the most part.

Tell me about cutting.

Ah, the elite of western world horsemanship.

No combination ever had such fun as man, horse and cattle beast.

In this free sport, where man is along for the ride, we are kings.

There is nothing like the dance in horse when the reins are swinging free.

This sport is very selective, and although many horses consider it as their physical purpose, not so many succeed due to difficulty in finding the right match in a human partner.

Tell me about ranch horses.

The worker bees in horse world.

See how they preserve the regal nature of horse, side by side with man, working toward common earth purpose.

This type of work requires sound mind and body that has hardiness in muscle, bone and thought.

Don't think for one moment it is not the greatest honour to have ranch work duties.

It is such a solid placement for horse, and the rewards in this occupation are countless, steeped in the grace of history with horse and Mankind.

I have done this, once or twice, so you know.

Tell me about reining.

The jive dancer of Horsedom.

See how glorious horse can be as he spins, cavorts and slides.

See especially how this horse does un-horse-like manoeuvres strictly for man's enjoyment and hysterical delight.

This sport has the most crowd appreciation, and the reining horse is addictive to all who watch him.

This industry has traditionally been harder on horse than expected due to age of participation.

Those who do it well love it.

Those who start too young burn out, and close their hearts off to save themselves.

They dream of another occupation but still try so hard.

It is the nature of horse to try for Mankind, and this particular aspect of occupation is troublesome for some.

Tell me about lesson horses.

The Saints of industry.

Blessed among horses for bringing so many into the world of horse.

A difficult occupation demanding tolerance of learning hands, seats and legs.

These horses are gemstones.

This occupation demands expertise in so many fields, and the horse that excels has great rewards in spirit.

No horse is alone in their travail, ever.

Tell me about three-day-eventing horses.

The skill required to excel at three disciplines takes an exceptional character of horse.

Few think twice when given the option of a superior contract in this field, as it is considered the most challenging of character and physical apparatus of horse.

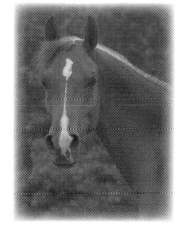

It is also the most fun endeavor under English saddlery, so expect those that come into this field and excel have large contracts to do so.

This particular field of performance sees shortening of physical duration due to demand, but horse accepts this as a rule and hurries with his other obligations within the guise of an eventer.

Tell me about gaited horses.

These little, industrious workers choose the challenge of going against normal Horsedom, and love twisting their bodies into peculiar positions for the appreciation of Mankind.

Troubled by the imposition of abnormal leg and gait, they still manage to endear so many in their efforts to jazz up the timing and elevation of limbs and feet.

It takes its toll on body only when added impositions out-balance the horse's effort to be balanced in an already unbalanced, un-horse like manoeuvre.

Trust that these horses are the acrobats and jugglers of Horsedom, but still love the circus in spite of the complications in their contracts.

Tell me about pack horses.

These represent the still thinkers of Horsedom, having chosen what appears to many to be a most boring existence, carrying lifeless baggage down seasoned trails on a continuous, monotonous basis.

They spend their mental and spiritual energies doing other things, while physical walks the trails repeatedly.

Trust that their lives are rich because of their other aspects, not represented by physical.

There is always a packer that has a heart in the horse that carries, regardless of weather or weight, with a dignity not befitting the environment.

It is this that strikes a chord with Mankind, the willingness to do the most mundane work for little reward, and the odd carrot.

Tell me about circus horses.

Ah yes. One of my favorites.

This stage takes a very special character to endure the highs and lows of show business.

The applause and the drudgery of travel seem balanced in the middle by hooking the fascination of millions of people into believing in the magic of horse.

It is not an easy position, being strictly an entertainer with little actual interaction with those millions, but trust that the heart-hooks of circus life have a base in the creatures that work there.

These horses never tire of the flamboyant demonstrations, in spite of mindless circles which form the base of their training.

It takes an exceptional character to be so focused, but see how they are remembered long after the circus has moved on.

Coach and driving horses.

The historic magic and timelessness of romance is carried in this occupation.

The horses that excel here have been in the history books in actuality, and the memories are carried energetically forward in them.

It is a most interesting phenomenon that when Mankind steps into the carriage he feels transported into another time and place.

This feeling of time travel comes from the horse itself, and is an addictive charge for Mankind when he feels it.

Thus, the carriage horse will always be a prominent choice for performance, and trust that it will always fascinate the one who drives and rides it.

Bucking horses.

Now we get to the fun part.

Never, in all of time, was there such a devoted, gleeful surge as in the bucking horse.

Every kick and roar carries with it the objections of Horsedom, as horse is free to demonstrate here.

See horse scream at historical mistreatment, thrust it with his heels, and project it into timeless banishment for eternity.

It is not that this horse suffered mistreatment, it is that he has the honour of kicking it so powerfully out of history, and he revels in that honour, giving every ounce of his power and prowess to do so.

This horse represents an elevation of athleticism that is rarely appreciated by other occupations.

But let them try to do this half as well as the true bucking horse.

I have thought of only a few occupations. More to say about that?

Yes. No doubt Mankind can think of many uses for our kind.

We are adaptable and came to assist.

Many work in individual homes and stables for the pleasure of being one-on-one with people.

It is our highest calling, the one-on-one-man-ship.

It requires dedication of a different sort - more intimate and heart to heart.

While working horses do commit their hearts for the most part to the people they know, the deepest heart relationships are saved for the caregivers who give back to the horses.

These may be the people in the background that are loved more than others.

It is always clear who the horse loves and who the horse just works for.

Tell me about retirement.

Some of us need it, some of us don't.

We appreciate being useful until our physical apparatus is useless for any purpose.

See usefulness in us, and we will outstay most other friendships for you.

Knowing your spiritual side more clearly now, how do we justify making you do work that sounds boring?

It is a natural part of horse purpose to do mundane things along with Mankind.

We accept that fully and have no regrets about the task at hand, as long as we see it assisting our purpose in the long run.

If the work you ask of us is not leading up to our purpose in contract, we will have more difficulty complying.

Know how accepting we are, and how hard we try to please, all in order to win your hearts and take you deeper than you thought horse was about.

See horse as Gift to you, and you will have no trouble seeing what is actually mundane to us.

We are so good at expressing our talent to you.

Don't leave us unattended on a walker, for our purpose is to show you what we have learned in the experience and interact vividly with you, present with us.

Left to ourselves, all exercise is pointless and boring.

We came to be with man.

Be with us, and our appreciation will know no bounds in training.

We wish to tell you clearly - we will do the circles and do the walker and do the boring around-the-arena-again exercise with you, if your heart is in the thing you ask.

If your heart is not in it, why on earth should ours be?

That is the best indicator of worthwhile effort.

Where is your heart in the process?

Trust that ours will be with yours in the doing of our work together.

Chapter Six

Equipment and other unmentionables

Tell me about bits.

Being clanged in the teeth is a barbaric practice.

We look at bits and wince for the most part.

Imagine wearing one yourself and hoping and praying your bit handler had good hands.

For the most part, bits are way more severe than is necessary for controlling us, and nothing sours a horse faster than a cruel bit.

Lifelong objectionable behaviors are founded with bits.

Once we learn to avoid the bit by head jerking or flipping over backwards, we consistently repeat the behavior that gave us relief.

Do your horses a favour and examine the bit you use.

Imagine wearing it loose or tight, or at all.

It is easy to know what we think about it this way, as we will transmit our feelings most powerfully on this count.

Tell me about crops, whips and sticks.

Oh my.

There you have it, the three most brutal wands in history.

Never did we deserve these tools, as we love to move forward, up and down and sideways.

Ask us nicely, seeing the end product, and you will be amazed what can be done without the mere mention of a stick.

Spurs.

Never mention these to me again.

A method to brutalize horses.

Tell me about trailers.

The trailer is a necessary evil for many horses.

The rides stress our legs, minds and bodies.

Uncertainty is difficult to overcome because we rarely understand the length of the journey.

For some of us the trailer is as good as home, if we have positive experiences with our people.

For others it is a death trap machine.

Personally it has never brought me much pleasure, but I endure it as requested.

Every attempt for comfort should be made in this department.

How do you like to stand in a trailer?

Personally, I like to see where I am going.

Others may prefer not looking.

And I mean that how it sounds - can't watch!

Just see that we have soft mats, fresh hay and fresh air.

We cope from there.

Tell me about long trips.

The effort is generally worth it for the partnership with our people.

Make every effort to see to our constant comfort.

It is difficult to justify the trip if the discomfort outweighs the positive benefits.

We remember long agonizing trips and think twice before embarking on another one.

For many horses, travelling is a normal event and becomes mundane, but not all horses travel so much that they dismiss it as normal for them.

Tell me about saddles in general.

Torture, if not a good fitting.

Add a rider's weight to a bad fitting saddle and you have a recipe for disaster.

We cannot perform if our back hurts or shoulders feel pinched.

Pair this idea with a rider seated forward on their seat bones, or unbalanced - worse than torture.

A good fitting saddle is the number one essential ingredient for performance to an excellent degree.

Dante and Cathy Seabrook, D.V.M.

All reasonable attempts to own a superior saddle should be made, and will be appreciated in depth by your horse.

Tell me how to saddle up.

This experience is dull and accepted for the most part half-heartedly.

It reeks of work, and initially many horses are sour when they see the thing.

Part of our sourness is related to the many ill-fitting pieces of tack that we are required to wear.

Squished shoulders are the bain of a bad saddle.

We think of all these things as you saddle up, and try to embellish our behavior to suit our thoughts about our saddle.

Twitching tails is a classic saddle gesture.

What about the type of saddle pad?

Crucial as well.

Thick, soft and toasty is best.

What about tie downs?

Shuts off our opinions.

Do you really not want to hear what we have to say about our situation?

If so, put a tie down on us.

What about hackamores?

We love these things.

The best scenario for co-operative expression.

Many horses' deep appreciation for this is profoundly evident to their people.

64

Any more to say about the equipment we use on you?

We wish man to know we accept this for the most part.

If you see us objecting by tossing our noses, slobbering all over our mouth, or bleeding from the spur, try to see it from our perspective please.

Something has gone amiss to cause these things, and trust that horse has tried to comply with your asking, but your asking was unclear to us.

Know we try for the most part to not only get along, but excel at what you are asking us.

If we haven't got it, you never knew how to ask correctly.

There is such potential for brutality with tools and mechanics used on horses, and all because you rushed into your idea of what we should be with you, instead of gently explaining what you wanted, or at least showing us in your mind.

If your mind is unclear, how are we to get it?

Many people working with horses have minds that look blank to us, as everything but the moment with us is in there.

Now we are working blind, so to speak, in deciphering what you want.

The greatest piece of equipment is your mind with us, as you are with us.

If you could sharpen your mind to be so clear in pictures at least, and send us a pre-view of what we are to do with you, it would surprise even the most diehard by-the-book trainer in the world.

Perfect example of a book on training but you never taught us to read.

There you have horse opinion, as mild as I can state it, on equipment used on horse.

Chapter Seven
Horse Senses

Just for fun, tell me about our assessment of your field of vision.

Well, you have it mostly right.

We can't see the top of our tail.

But as far as depth perception, we are feeling the energy of the thing too, and how deep the puddle is is not the issue.

There is energy in water that we are reading as rapidly as possible before we step in it or through it.

The water came from elsewhere and brings stories.

If it is moving water we are interpreting those stories very quickly.

So it is not about how deep the water is.

It's will I step in these stories or not take part.

Can you focus clearly on our face in front of you?

Oh yes, every pore.

And we love every pore.

Are some horses short-sighted?

No, because we are all seeing in a different way.

I am teasing a bit here, because I interpret short-sighted as the seeing on the spiritual journey.

We are far-sighted beings.

Tell me about your sense of smell.

Such a gift God gave us here, allowing us to read every creature and thing on the planet.

Everything has its own smell, so distinct and telling of its own story.

We delight in this sense with such total glee.

We even smell the kind of day you had at work on you - what you endured, what you enjoyed, what you breathed out.

Give us your hand in offering and we will smell your day for you, and help you accordingly.

How good is your sense of smell?

Only dogs rival us.

We smell from such distance, aided by wind.

Can you smell water?

No.

We sense it by the energy it stores.

It also calls to us in a way difficult to explain, as a security from Nature for continuance.

Water has a sound we are more likely to hear, and birds that sing its presence to us.

What's your favorite smell?

It is you.

More?

Hay is a specialty.

Other horses too.

Can you smell treats in pockets?

Most of them.

The scent is always on you as well from putting them there.

Do you smell death?

We sense it in the being that died.

If it is past the sweetness in the lingering, we smell decomposure.

It does not bother us, but interests us in the event somewhat.

Do you smell fear on people?

Of course not - we feel it.

It is in the vibration around the person, and in their eyes.

If they ride us now we feel it in their seat and hands, and it is always amplified in a fearful rider.

Nothing hides it there.

Are some smells obnoxious to horse?

Diesel, gasoline and other solvents.

Strong chemical smell will get us wondering, but not enough to feel the need to leave the area.

Tell me about flehmen response.

This particular exhibition represents total lostness in the moment, reading thoroughly every minute detail in the air that brings the smell to us.

Stallions are so absorbed in their mating duties that this inhaling of story of Mare about incapacitates him.

It is true this time may be a moment he is catchable, when any other time he is not.

So much information, like downloading your entire computer contents and having to decipher it all in mere minutes - this is a reasonable comparison of behavior to flehmen.

So how good is your hearing?

With intention to hear halfway round the world, we can.

The reason is, we hear with ears and we hear with heart.

So our ears hear clearly all the wind brings from five miles around us - really.

Our heart hears more generally worldwide.

For instance, we are fully aware of horse circumstances in Europe from here.

We hear the stories of magnificence of soul.

We hear the stories of sad abuse.

We hear of Mankind's commitment to horse, and animals, and earth.

Truth be told, we try to hear loudest the good news, and prefer the bad to whisper to us.

Do some horses go deaf?

Rarely.

It always accompanies misuse of noise around the horse on such a constant basis, that horse prefers to block it out, and other sound goes with the blocking.

Gunshots are a perfect example.

Why would horse endure that noise, which is worse than a sonic boom in our excellent performing ears?

Just stop hearing, and then use the feeling of sound as our hearing, and the hearing of heart for what is really important.

Do you appreciate human music?

Sometimes.

Sometimes it is also grating on our ears and skin.

We feel sound abruptly when it booms or screeches.

Radios making background noise are little comfort to us, as we have our own preference in music.

And what is that?

The wind brings us the music of the world, from the leaves in the trees to the grass on the ground.

It all makes sound that comforts us in the deepest resonance of well-being.

Nothing like the sound of dirt, or trees, or rock, or field.

This is difficult to comprehend for you, this *feeling* of sound, but it is how we know the presence of All-That-Is is right here with us on our journey.

Stars also make music, even harder for you to imagine.

The moon and the sun have songs in the light they give, with light and sound as one.

Sometime man may hear this feeling, and feel this hearing.

Hard at present with so much noise going on in this time and space.

Wind. What is wind to horse?

The master Story Teller, the master Gifter of reasons to endure.

It brings us life from faraway places - tales of magnificence, tales of woe, and consistency of life on the planet.

We read it, we hear it, we smell it, and we run with it.

What joy is in wind for horse!

I often think on a windy day the ride will be challenging.

Yes, we are so busy interpreting, reading, smelling, and wanting to bolt with wind.

You are so right.

Do you like our singing?

Not so much, but it helps your state of calm with us.

That strikes me quite funny - I always thought you liked my singing!

We prefer our own noise to yours, naturally.

Tell me the meaning of different horse sounds.

The nicker...

Come here, you might be getting into trouble over there - to foal.

Or, welcome, friend, I have been waiting.

If mare says it, it means the first.

To send this to people is a complement, just so you know.

The neigh...

Where are you guys?

The high loud snort...

There! Finished! Ta-dah!

The soft blowing out your nose...

Now I've got it, whew...

Some of you have very musical voices.

Yes, we are all different.

See how Regalo calls to you in his Spanish voice because he knows you love that.

We are not indifferent to appreciation on any level you see.

Do you like bells and jingles?

Not really.

Any unnatural noise we tolerate as part of general life and work.

But we prefer the sound of the earth moving in space, and all that entails.

Can you hear radio waves or cell phone waves?

No. But we feel them.

They come in literal waves on the air and these are palpable to horse.

It is something else we adjust to.

City horses are bombarded with air waves, and somehow tolerate it in time.

How good is your hearing?

At least ten times what man's is.

Keen beyond most domesticated creatures.

Always consider that when you train us.

A chirp is a blast of racket to horse's ears, that's why we scoot when we hear it.

Do some noises physically hurt your ears?

Yes - loud, high-pitched sounds reverberate for ages in our sensitive ears.

Many horses cannot tolerate loud noises of intense high pitch.

Is it true your ear and eye point together to the thing you are concentrating on?

Yes. Focused concentration reads so much more.

Yet we are also able to direct them separately in some situations, for example, when I must watch ahead of me more intently, but you command from the saddle, and now ear and eye are not in concert.

It just depends on the moment.

Tell me how powerful your sense of feel is.

Now we come to the most profound sense of all.

We feel your energetic touch.

We feel touch coming at us in the bushes, thus the reason we watch so closely.

We feel your breathing touch, your hand over our energetic field touch, and your visual touch.

Watch how your focus on us has an energy we respond to.

Why do you think we watch so closely when you get intent?

It is because we have *felt* your look, as we feel sound.

Yes, the fly is there with his tender little feet, but we felt him there inches before he landed.

Buzzing flies create a tickling of sorts in the energetic space around them.

We sense all of this profoundly.

So what do you think we feel in a slap, or a pat, or a mane pulling?

Of course these are amplified way past human comparison.

Tell me about the horse we call dull to cues.

This horse has decided to tone it down because he chooses not to respond to excessive stimulation from people.

He will withstand the spur and the drag on his mouth, going elsewhere in those moments in his mind.

These horses are asking you to learn a powerful lesson about politeness, at the cost of their literal hide.

They ask you to think how to motivate someone unmotivate-able.

Now you have to really think, because the physical burden you place on this horse he can ignore.

Here is your contract with this "dull" horse, to use your excellent mind to carve a new idea to do with him that is the kindest, sweetest idea your brain has ever had about a horse.

And once you find that creative, soft, sweet asking of horse, he will become the most responsive, soft, sweet ride you have ever known.

We see lots of horses missing skin from other horses telling them to move. How does that feel?

These horses had to state their opinion of their position in the band clearly.

Sure, it smarts to have skin removed.

But simply weigh the benefit of the bullies leaving you alone if you ignore their picking on you, and now you have relative peace in your pasture life that would have been denied you had you run away to avoid it.

Tell me about taste for horses.

We already know sugar is the supreme treat.

We taste less acutely than our other senses, but enough to give us great pleasure eating good horse food.

Many of us taste chemicals and drugs as bitter and obnoxious, although some horses accept anything given by hand with an overruling expectation of tasting good, so the surprise of an icky taste is quickly forgotten.

We have trouble detecting badness in feed, due to some tolerance of taste once it is spread out and diluted.

Some horses object to a different brand of molasses, while others cannot detect it.

It may be said best, that the most sensitive horses will have adverse taste pronounced in their experience, and other less sensitive horses will eat just about anything regardless of its taste.

And of course we have preferences in our feed, knowing what we really prefer to eat, given the choice.

Some medicines try to taste like strawberries for you.

This is hopeless and futile.

Nothing overcomes the chemical taste.

Like aspirin for you, try chewing it and see if it is masked by anything you butter it with.

Would you call spirit-purpose-knowing your sixth sense?

Not a bad title per se.

We love how man names things, and this is one of your cutest expressions.

What is sixth sense to horse?

It is God-speak in us.

It is the eternal knowing of the eternal being of us, of Horse and Horse-Man.

It is in the overpowering veto of anything one could call bad, if bad really deserved attention.

It is in the knowing that at the base of All-That-Is, all is really and truly well, and that such a profound inrushing hurricane of Grace comes at man, and horse is along for this brilliant ride of this physical life with you, our hearts swelling with the thing that defies language and outdoes all attempts to describe it - the weak, little, tiny word called love.

There, you have it.

Chapter Eight
Memory

Tell me about horse memories.

We have precision memories, all of us.

Necessary for survival and growing in purpose.

Not all of us choose to keep some of those memories and are able to shelve them essentially into a minute space that we rarely then if ever reference.

Some memories do not serve us in recovery times.

Other horses never forget one thing, and every time you work with them, it seems you try to overcome the same darn episode that triggers flight-ready response in horse.

Just honour the thing that did it to us; just say how you appreciate our brilliant capacity to never forget what was really important in our lives.

Now, just go about our business together, accepting the behavioral result of that thing, embracing our memory of it.

It gives it permission to fade when you say, "I appreciate how quickly you respond when I turn these clippers on, and your reaction time is so excellent!"

I am using a mild example here – well…mild for some horses.

This is appreciation for my excellence of flight readiness.

Now, as odd as it seems, I can energetically relax about the thing in appreciation of it.

Now, we are better.

It is simple energetic math, add good energy to the bad event, and now it becomes a zero.

Try it!

Would you tell me some memories as a foal?

No. That's a secret.

Ok. Any memories you would be able to share?

Yes. I remember hope.

It kept me sane even when it was misplaced, so to speak.

The night sky held it for me best, and I remember the moon and myself understanding my contract, as if we had a secret that only we knew.

It was my peaceful time, with the moon.

Do you remember your mother?

Of course.

She was a brood mare in a large stable.

She had sad eyes from so many babies taken from her too young.

She taught me fast, as she knew she had little time.

She also knew I had greater purpose than most foals she had had.

She warned me my journey would be full of difficulty in the beginning, but it would prepare me for such a life journey that I would not regret a moment of the preparation.

So your mother knew your story?

Of course, deep within.

Our hearts speak too, you know.

More on mother?

I miss her still, yet miss her not, as she is fully present with me.

That's spirit for you.

Difficult for me to explain fully.

Do you talk with her in some way?

She is in spirit fully now, and yes I can.

Mostly we experience the thing in feeling together and no speaking is required or necessary for understanding.

Did you know your sire?

No, I never knew him.

He was an ancient sort, and rather famous I understand.

This relationship is distant to me, but yes I will know him fully once this life is done here.

Lessons Mother taught you.

"Be ready to endure for great cause. It will be alright darling."

These words I remember best.

Do you remember the people in other lifetimes?

No - too vague.

We always leave all but the positive growth in the past.

We do plant stars when love is our journey.

And if we are so blessed as to have an exceptional contract, now *that* we never forget.

It is as if we work toward the exception in all those lifetimes, and sort of earn our wings and right to participate at higher levels of purpose.

I like to think that if people love their horse that their horse never forgets them.

And in love stories this is true, so don't let that worry you.

In many lifetimes it was not about love stories, but there always was a story with healing and helping, and bonding.

Much of what horse did was simply not spoken of openly, as we were considered beasts of burden, or animals without soul.

The world is changing and ready to learn more now.

And this changes our stories too, because now love is the featured part of our relationship, and this love never dies - never, ever.

During a lifetime, details of a previous life are vague and deep in the background of our being.

When we return to pure spirit, the fullness of all stories is vivid and accessible.

This will help you understand why I can't remember and assure you that I will always remember you.

Such is the directive of our purpose.

Do previous lifetimes affect the present lifetime only for good?

Of course.

No sensible being would let negative associations tag along for the ride.

Nothing is ever lost, but nothing is carried forward that creates problems for the new time.

We only take the best forward, and the rest is put to bed, so to speak.

And blessed for the teaching of soul it brought.

Do you remember the name you were given before I found you?

Yes.

Can you share that with me?

No. I am Dante.

Chapter Nine
People in General

Tell me how it feels to be with people.

Complete in purpose.

Soft, and hard, and interesting.

Always making us think how to clearly communicate without words for the most part.

Always a study in patience and often tolerance.

Tell me about horses and women.

The fairer sex is also fair in mind to us.

We love horsewomen.

Their hearts for the most part are inviting and warm, and we do get away with some things, but it all endears us powerfully to women.

Most women are born with a desire to interact with horses.

Your blacksmith always kids about this, but it is true.

Horses don't prefer women over men, but more women than men prefer horses.

It is a most favorable match.

Tell me about men and horses.

This is where history comes in powerfully.

Together men and horses shaped the world.

Men had powerful ideas and horses were matched in powerful bodies.

Many men also had soft spots in their hearts for their mounts, but only horse knew this.

Today, men continue in their powerful relationship with horses, but speak about the heart part.

It is our greatest pride to hear their heart stories told.

Tell me about children.

We live for our experience with most children.

Little hearts are so open to horse.

It is true that there is a horse space in children's hearts, and filling it early establishes strength of character difficult to match otherwise.

We don't say this with pride as you know it, but with a deeper sense of accomplishment that is Heaven-based.

It is simply true.

Show them how to be safe around us, and then set them free to fly with us.

No parent ever regretted establishing a relationship with horse and children.

Only good can come of it.

Tell me what you think of the names we give you.

This puts us in hysterics, literally.

There is so much in a name, leaning energy to good or bad impressions.

Some of us detest our names, especially if they are negative-based.

Some of us have a callus where our name is concerned.

If given the chance, name us for the positive, name us for greatness intended, and name us for love.

If you name us Nitro, we will object by being like that.

If you name us Daisy, we will accede to the lovely flower's nature.

Who would you rather ride I ask?

Tell me why it feels so good to ride you.

We take you into your own power effortlessly.

We remind you of your powerful history and raise you up, not just physically, but mindfully and spiritfully.

There is no comparison riding anything else, because we give you the opportunity to be one with another creature, and Mankind seeks this oneness.

Tell me why it feels so good to be with you.

We are entertaining!

Seriously now, we heal worries for you.

We exact peace from the space we are in, and we don't mind sharing it with you.

You can feel this around us for the most part.

Tell me about horse heroes.

We have heroes that we appreciate for the positive change they effect worldwide for Horsekind.

But our biggest heroes are precious people acting out life with us on the backstage, so to speak, in the trenches with us.

We see heroes everywhere, unrecognized by others.

As for us, we are pleased to serve Mankind's purpose and appreciate positive attention, but it is all part of being horse and not really a choice for us to be otherwise.

Tell me about your part in wars.

We had little choice, being committed to man's journey so intimately.

We gave equally, selflessly.

It is our nature and right to participate where we feel it is necessary to be for the greatest effect in relationships.

Many hearts were supported in wars, and still are.

We care not what side we are on, only about the people we interact with.

Tell me about your part in healing.

Now we get to the nitty-gritty.

We are the Emotional Healers of all time and space.

Trust that one's involvement with horse cannot go undetected.

Something will change.

For many, hearts are healed, and minds are brightened.

We sense wounding in people and many of us are drawn to move it to Source for you.

We are able to take certain emotions and process them through us, into the ground.

It may be surprising to learn of this ability.

I like to say we turn it over to Mother Earth where it is changed into brilliant, white light.

I love that!

It is our greatest accomplishment, really.

Tell me about interactions with horse service people.

We are always challenged to deal with those who are not our people.

Always, as with you meeting caregivers that deliver discomfort, there is tension and apprehension.

We bear it, as there is little choice generally in the matter.

What kind of energy are you looking for in a farrier?

Complacent co-operator.

The quieter the better.

The more tolerant the better.

Remove the rasp as a tool of torture and we are happy.

Stretching our legs the way they are not meant to go creates our objections.

We do try to co-operate but sometimes it is not our day in our mind to have our feet done.

Oh, and don't forget to attend to flies so we can stand still.

That's my personal bug.

How do horses feel about being tied in a chute to have their feet done?

This is barbaric to most.

To some it is like death, not being able to move at all.

To some it is the only way horse will allow work done.

Some sort of balance needs to be attained here to save horse's minds about this.

We tend to lose some heart in this experience.

Tell me about horseshoes.

An aid in modern world foot-stepping.

Sometimes a dis-aid.

What in your opinion needs attention in your hooves?

Heel and toe.

Like the dance.

Address heel issues and shorten our toes some, and we can grow you a perfect foot, functional and strong.

Messing with our angles is a detriment and doing too little is as bad as doing too much.

What kind of energy are you looking for in a veterinarian?

The best of all energies.

This occupation demands our co-operation at times when we are virtually unable to co-operate.

Bring the best of thoughts to our encounters and the best of manners.

Tell us out loud or in mind what is going to be done to us, for we can't imagine it is in our best interest in the throes of our biology.

Later on we can assimilate it into our relationship, and if you have asked us nicely we will be better the next time.

If not, use your imagination about what we will do when you touch us, and you will not be mistaken.

We know who knows about horses and who knows about cows.

But we appreciate every effort to be reverent and honour all intention to treat us when it comes from a benevolent heart.

Heart will dismiss all perceived wrongs done to us.

How are we doing as a profession?

Not bad, considering your minds are slanted in the opposite direction in pure science, as a rule.

It is the exceptional veterinarian that begins to peruse spirit as a reason for disease, but in this day and age, presenting that to the owner is difficult and crosses the line between medicine and ministry.

We fully understand the plight of the considerate, spiritual veterinarian.

Just keep trying.

We will show our appreciation for your journey with us.

We have watched from your beginnings as humble, beyond-caregivers, and we have witnessed powerful, positive change in the veterinary field.

Veterinarians as a rule are such special people to us.

We look like we dread your visit, but in truth we understand and so appreciate all you do for horse and Animalkind.

Nothing goes unnoticed, and we try to maintain our sense of humour when we see you again.

What kind of energy are you looking for in a trainer?

We need someone who has indomitable focus.

Don't send us to someone who can't concentrate on us, or on the task at hand.

We will progress somewhat in the hands of a distracted trainer, but watch us go when you find someone who concentrates on us in the moment.

Pair that with gentleness of hand and heart, and it can't be beat.

Tell me about situations where horses are not cared for.

We expect some lifetimes will hold suffering, thus the types of horse journeys available for us to choose.

We do not hold Mankind responsible in hatred of his actions, but we do recognize injustice clearly and it stays in our hearts in some form.

There is no point in belabouring suffering; it is part of our journey with Mankind and we accept its status.

Often, this beginning place is the thing that effects powerful change within horse to interact with people who have suffered.

We are now matched in experience, in order to help both of us heal from it.

All suffering has purpose it seems.

Dante and Cathy Seabrook, D.V.M.

These horses that suffer neglect and abuse and slaughter - what about their contracts with Mankind?

Do not kid yourself for one moment that these horses in particular are not the most powerful horses on the planet.

They come with a Universal contract to effect change of such magnitude I can't describe it to you adequately.

Hearts melt at horse's condition.

Poster children horses are everywhere, with great purpose and knowing that because of their poster child choice, they get a fresh, loving start – here, or there.

Weep not for our situation, for we come fully prepared and knowledgeable of our purest intention.

If we look pathetic, it is only our biology.

Never forget that, and it will help you recover from our plight.

In chronic extreme neglect, some horses I interacted with seemed to me to have despair in their DNA. Comment?

They did.

It went so deep they were born with a knowing of having a pointless existence.

That so goes against horse Being that they could not leave it behind them when they escaped their circumstance.

These horses tried to embrace another life, but the difficulty was insurmountable for them.

They stayed true to the neglect embedded in their being.

One old mare I was treating thought the IV was poison. Is there really a point where spirit cannot overcome and the truth be known?

Good question.

You have come to the right place.

Of course spirit is all-powerful, truly.

Horse has a choice to believe or not.

Horse knows it has a choice.

This mare did not have time to believe in her right to choose.

She had been there in neglect so long, countless years in her mind, and it was difficult if not impossible to believe in the kindness of man after all this time.

Even I, going through five years waiting for you to find me, had to *powerfully intend to believe* it could be better, and I knew our story.

So see this poor old mare, never knowing kindness, and now she is subjected to veterinary procedures that remind her of her powerlessness in this life.

She needed way more time to come to grips with the fact that you were trying to help, not further her misery.

Is this another situation where the character of the horse determines the depth charge of the neglect?

Neglect has one face for all.

Tell me about horse slaughter.

A burden too miserable to devote much thought to.

We accept this result of unconsciousness of this time.

It must be borne.

Horses here reconsider if they will return, or stay in pure spirit timelessly.

Many people are sick at heart about this. How can we help?

Lobby against it if possible.

Otherwise see us whole and brilliant as we are, but let us endure it for you.

We are that capable.

Think about it on the many levels it represents, and you will see Mankind is leaning heavily in the right direction.

Tell me about wishing it were better for you.

Here is the place that is the most powerful to effect change for Horsekind.

Seeing something that disagrees with your perception of our treatment, and wishing it were different has merit, and often all you can do is send us a wish for that particular circumstance.

The wish is powerful indeed, changing the energy for us, sometimes in that life situation, or sometimes in our next life situation.

For example, you wished for Shakespeare to be well and happy and appreciated, which he could not accomplish his last lifetime, but this time he has all the benefits of your wishing, for which he is endlessly thankful.

So wish us better in the plight you see us in, and it will change things for us, one lifetime or another.

It is the same for all Animalkind, this power to wish it better.

If you could only see it for what it really is, a possibility for something better, it would ease your suffering about our suffering.

Tell me about God.

Where do I begin?

We are fused together with God in purpose, clarity and love.

We act from His benevolence.

We love from His heart.

We see with His eyes your beautiful spirits, and the rest is just pale in comparison.

Our biology makes it so much more fun than being invisible demonstrating these qualities of God, so we come with powerful intention to play with you.

God loves this play.

So you feel spiritual awe and inspiration from horse, as God energy is infused in our being, and playing with us too.

It is an incomparable dance with God that we share with you freely.

Not one soul need miss out.

What are your words for God?

All-That-Is, Source, God.

The words for God are irrelevant and used as an all encompassing term for the eternal word-defying thing that loves, understands and holds you in Grace unimagined.

Multiply this by the millionth degree and there is a beginning place for you.

These words are a good start, but so insufficient.

God out-languages every tongue.

Tell me about forgiveness.

We, like God, have the capacity to look at Mankind in a way that recognizes nothing to forgive.

Your intention at your base core to be your full God-version of you is what we see looming hugely in our vision.

This overpowers little things, and all things are "forgivable".

It is our nature to forgive, as you call it, but we don't think about it like that.

We appreciate all attempts to do better the next time, and even the smallest degree of try is fully celebrated by horse.

We don't bear grudges, but we do know better than to go through an uncomfortable experience again if it can be avoided.

We have excellent memories, which serve us well so we survive the next time the lion attacks.

We see minute details, and read your energy perfectly.

Every reaction by horse is refreshed with new attempts, and no ill will is thought.

But we perceive your intentions fully as we read your energy coming at us, and being very sensitive and intelligent creatures, we do what we feel is best in the situation to avoid further discomfort.

It is not that we dislike some people, or hate some things; we read the energy which is so discordant from our core energy and we choose to avoid it if possible.

There, tolerance of a degree immeasurable comes into play, as we can't always avoid the energy that is like squeaking chalk to our ears.

Tell me about love.

At last, something very worthy to speak about.

Love - the reason horses choose to come as horses.

We are love itself in heart and soul, and our journey with you is only about that.

For love we accept all you do to us, all you want to do with us and all the baggage you present in our confrontations.

We will take anything you intend us to take, and often what you have no idea we can take.

Think about it for a moment and you will remember a change in how you felt with a horse.

What was that? Was it our shiny coats or quizzical expressions that got to you?

No, it was an energetic relief as we absorbed your stuff and dissipated it into the vapours.

You don't have to ask if we love you, but ask how we love you and explore how deeply we are able to reach to show it.

This is the reality, that horse can take your emotional energy and direct and diffuse it away from you, and it will transform into something beneficial.

You can request it and hold the intention that we will take it as you ride or work with us, or we can take it on all by ourselves without being asked.

Often, maybe generally, people simply have no idea about what we really do, they just know they feel better riding or working with their horse.

This love goes further as we help ground you in your life experiences away from us.

We are knowing creatures and understand your trials more deeply than you can imagine.

Trust that we do all we can in many invisible ways to uphold you in your trials and tribulations of regular life.

This is important to speak of as it will help many when they ask purposefully for us to take the thing that troubles them energetically, and of course we are so happy to do this in love.

Chapter Ten

Other Animals and Horse

Tell me about consciousness in animals.

Well, you see the beginnings of horse here, with a consciousness rivalling Mankind's, truly.

Within the horse being, there are different levels of consciousness per se, depending on one's contract, one's measured trips to earth in lifetimes, one's endurance challenges, and one's individual situation with Mankind.

For example, it does not take a supreme level of consciousness to pull a cart, but it does take a different level to pull the cart to earn the man his living.

So no horse is without recognition of the higher good in the situation, and is always aware of the depth of perception required in the moment.

But many horses have deep contracts with Mankind.

Deep, individual contracts require higher levels of consciousness, as you call it, in those contracts.

It is just exactly like in people, where some individuals are real go-getters and some are seemingly on simpler levels of life.

See how horse is matched to their contracts on consciousness required there.

Higher contracts, higher consciousness, but always a level of brilliance in consciousness of horse, which is not mimicked elsewhere in the animal kingdom.

What other animals seem to rank higher in consciousness, as we call it?

You have thought of dolphin, elephant, dog, cat, and ape.

However, see the consciousness in Eagle, as he demonstrates the purity of freedom and makes Mankind wish to soar with him, and see the magnificence of Whale, as he rules the ocean in a softness belying his size, and see the Lion as he enchants man in his stare from eyes that go back into the centuries of time.

All animals have significant consciousness, (your word), significant empowering in their Beings, and none are little in God's estimation.

Tell me about your ideas on dogs.

Dogs fulfill great purpose too, in a different way of course.

We get along splendidly as a rule, unless the dog goes awry of purpose.

Many dogs befriend horses and take an active role in combination with us and people.

They revel in side-by-side travel with us, knowing nothing better than a good exploration at our side.

It is a delicate friendship we hold, being opposites in thought.

We run, they chase.

Funny how this dance involves no tolerance, only pure acceptance of another brilliant being.

Tell me about cats.

Cats are a different story.

Cats tell us their secrets.

We are such good listeners too.

Many a lonely night has been spent in the company of cat narration.

Many energies are transmuted through cats, different from horses, but related to broader spectrum energies in people's lives.

So less specific as a rule, but very beneficial.

We get along well with cats generally, and sometimes they are our only conversation in the day that we speak out loud.

What about sheep?

This gentle creature suffers our company.

We appreciate their attempt to entertain us, and we bear them no ill will.

Sometimes the combination is not so favorable and we do damage together, although it is not meant to be that way.

A sheep is a good temporary friend for many, but the degree of companionship leaves us wanting.

Tell me about goats.

Now there's a creature made famous in our history as a milk-maid for foals.

Arrogant little beings that are most entertaining in character and behavior generally.

We meld together well when horse is an infant, and appreciate the contribution to our well being.

Tell me about llamas and horses.

A rich tapestry of mind here, with only forward progress related to growth of thought together.

This creature holds deep insight, and we are both appreciative of time spent in energetic discussion and opinion.

Tell me about the cattle.

We came, many of us, with purpose with cattle.

Mankind could not do without us in this field.

We still love to interact in areas of great working purpose, and it reminds us of our deep commitment to Mankind's path.

There was never more fun than the dance with the cow.

Mind on mind, eye on eye, and keen anticipation ruling the dance.

For their part, cattle know us as different skilled beings, come with separate purpose than themselves, with both contributing to man's existence brilliantly.

Tell me about birds and horses.

The birds are our sentinels.

Many stories are told in the trees and we understand them fully.

Sometimes when we seem to dance with upset energy it is from the conversation in the birds.

They see all from their vantage point on high and have been warning us for centuries of danger and disruption.

We have a symbiotic dance it seems, and accept birds as the gentle message bearers they are, so closely, very closely linked to Source support.

Tell me about lions and tigers and bears.

You would ask me this!

Of course we, none of us, wish to be eaten.

But we understand the prey-predator dance, and dance it is, if you could only see it that way.

The balance of nature is maintained through this dance.

It is give and take of such a high degree, that Mankind has trouble with the concept.

Of course we run from the lion, and hopefully we outrun him and give him thought.

But if he catches us, there is a blocking of the terror that would overcome us, and a lifting into the hands of God prior to our last gasps.

If you could understand the benevolence of our Creator, you would know there is no suffering in the nature dance, however it appears to you.

The biology remains to go through the offering of prey to predator, and it puts up a good show.

But spirit and mind are occupied with other matters, higher matters, in conversation with God about our re-emergence and celebration once back as pure, positive, spirit energy.

It is most difficult to comprehend how we look compared to how we feel.

If you could pretend you see God there in the act of prey gift to predator, you could begin to understand the grace in the dance of nature.

Just trust that we know that lions and tigers and bears are also important to nature, and long before the world began, we agreed to the dance.

Chapter Eleven

When Physical Demonstrates Spiritual

Tell me about diseases.

Deadly diseases have a purpose.

We honour all life and take part in the dance.

Most horses that die from diseases have purpose included in their illness in order to encourage development for the greater whole.

Vaccines are an example.

Like in humans, diseases accompany negativity, and chronic negativity plagues horses in their occupations.

It makes us susceptible whereas in the wild we only deal with nature, and are less prone to be set up for disease to enter.

We have an accepting attitude towards nature and her other commitments.

Why are horses more susceptible to some diseases, like Tetanus and West Nile virus?

Again, we are such sensitive souls!

The nature of our Being's purpose is to delve into energy matters, and our capability to help you with your emotions, yet not take them for ourselves, leaves our systems open and welcoming to some things we would rather not invite to the party.

So we are sensitive to some biological things that come in the back door, so to speak, because of our gifts to aid you in emotional healing.

We accept it as part of the package, because there is way more good in this ability than bad.

It's all relative.

Tell me about injuries and ailments.

Big one here.

We often choose our ailments to demonstrate our resistance to an event or way of life.

It is all we have to object with.

When the objectionable article is removed, we can easily return to full function, generally.

Sometimes we choose long standing issues for the growth of our person, or people.

We consider injuries a normal part of negotiation and demonstration, because few of us have opportunity to really speak up.

I personally have used this to avoid attending clinics.

You figured it out on the last one and gave me permission to object without injury.

Thank-you.

Do you choose specifically the injury?

Not specifically, but generally.

It depends on the situation but there is symbolic significance to the injury.

For example, a leg injury signifies that horse does not want to move forward in the direction he was being taken.

A lung or breathing issue is related to squashing of the spirit purpose at that time and space.

Most injuries are redeemable, but not all.

Some stay as reminders to not go so deep the next time.

Going too deep, giving too much of spirit, damages the integrity of that horse's purpose that lifetime.

If he gives too much there is nothing left.

Horse is an absorbent being, meaning we take on energies about our circumstances sometimes too freely, resulting in physical changes.

As far as emotions go, we hold firm and do not absorb your troubles, but if our spirit journey and highest purpose is blocked to us, then our physical bodies reflect the difficulty we encountered.

Does it have to be a significant event?

It generally is.

We don't fool around with damaged tissue unless there is great purpose or distraction required in the moment.

We don't choose injury willy-nilly; it is carefully considered prior to taking it on.

So for clarity and understanding, does every injury or disease have purely a spiritual base, or partly a spiritual base?

All things have a spiritual base.

Not one thing is an exception.

The degree of expression does relate to the character of the horse, how he came as horse and how deep his purpose with the person or people is.

For instance, everything you and I do is pure spiritual.

Everything a silly horse does is not going to indicate a deep spiritual drive to show you he is frustrated with his path, as this horse does not know frustration.

If he injures himself, he was more likely silly than seriously showing you his lack of direction.

So you must look to the type of horse and the type of relationship he is in.

If he is in deep, deep purpose with Mankind then all physical manifestations are symbolizing the spirit journey and an expression of his whereabouts with himself and his person.

Are injuries or diseases taken on solely for growth in the person?

No, not all, although you grow when we show you our opinion of ourselves in our journey with you.

It is like a self-regulating control button.

If we stray from what we set out and intended for our lifetime, a deeper we, from the purest part of us, makes sure we demonstrate physically the upset in our purpose that we then notice, and then within ourselves we are checked and can re-direct our actions and thoughts in the right direction again.

The contracts are binding in a way difficult to comprehend, but they are bound by threads of Heaven if you will, that nothing can break.

Is it correct to say then that some injuries are for our growth, and some are reminders for horse that he is distracted from true purpose and time to get back on track?

Yes, you have it now.

And does the thing that stimulates the injury or disease have to be a chronic thing, or could it be a one-time thing that sets it in motion?

It is always somewhat chronic.

There is sufficient expanse to horse that we can withstand the beginnings, and some of us notice it then and do something about it.

But if we are younger in teaching regarding spirit journeys, or just too busy to notice the little suggestions, the stimulus will build up a bit before we see the physical demonstration that reminds us we strayed off track.

So there are young and old spirit journeys?

The Being of the individual horse may have not had so many lifetimes to build up really significant teaching knowledge.

We all begin somewhere.

Some choose only a few lifetimes, some choose many.

Obviously the more the merrier.

Seriously, the more we come back, the more we expand in knowledge about how clever it is possible to be aiding man in our journey together.

Pretty simple arithmetic.

I, as you know, am ancient.

If we have trouble figuring out the answer to the injury, does it matter?

Never. Eventually you will understand.

If you have the opportunity to be studying with a powerful mentor, understanding will come quicker.

If you study with a powerful mentor, expect more symbology to emerge.

If the opportunity for you to grow in spirit understanding is available, we will jump at the chance to involve you.

Colic. We dread this word for you.

Some of us are so brilliant that we are pretty quick to demonstrate waywardness, like colic-ing horses.

Colic is never our first choice of objection.

It is pretty serious if we choose colic as our method of objection demonstration.

Colic is an expression of temporary disgust at our circumstance.

Sometimes it is our choice of venue to re-emerge into pure spirit.

We look awful in the throes of colic, but God is sparing spirit throughout, and truly, in the great scheme of things, we, the full being of we, are able to partly separate from the demonstration, and wait it out thinking of other things to do when the ruckus is over.

So what would make a horse disgusted?

Sometimes we misjudge a situation in our purpose.

We are not perfect you know, and we do learn a bit as we go along.

Some situations just make us feel a little sick for how things are going, and in our attempt to correct a line of direction we end up chastising ourselves and self-condemnation always gives us a gut ache.

That makes perfect sense to me.

Of course it does.

If we see you are in serious medical trouble like colic, what is the best way to be of assistance to you?

Call for chemical help for us if possible.

We will deal with the spirit aspect of causing our gut ache, but most horses need and appreciate some assistance managing the pain we caused.

When I first met you, you had a glorious mane and tail which was cut off before I could speak up for you, and you never grew it back. Tell me why.

It was too representational of my life experience before you came.

It was the only glory in my being.

Now, the glory is in every hair in a different way.

No need for a big mane and tail.

More clarity to offer here?

Simply said, everything means something deeper.

Nothing is without a reason.

Look at your horse and consider, could this be a symbol of something in our journey, or do I have this silly, funny-face horse that tripped over the wheelbarrow.

It will be easier than you think.

Honour all thoughts regarding the spiritual base of disease and injury.

You can't miss them when they hit you.

You will feel puzzled about a situation, and the clue is that the physical demonstration will feel weird, bizarre or baffling.

If you get those feelings, check for spiritual teachings in disease.

Now, we are complete on that.

Are there any accidents?

Not really.

We have an inner knowing about accomplishing our purpose and have many choices in the moment, all considered carefully in the blink of a blink of an eye.

Spirit decisions have speed unheard of.

What looks like it took seconds to occur here was reviewed in energy prior, and the horse is prepared in spirit for what looks like an unexpected occurrence in body and mind.

Emotions are always expressed, regardless of prior knowledge; that is a rule of horse performance.

So you see our emotional-physical-mental reaction in the event, but know that spirit has understood and had choice fully in it.

There is always a reason, but it may take deep searching in the moment to find it, and later it surfaces effortlessly in your mind and brings you at least some understanding of the purpose of the event.

I would say most accidents have nothing to do with horse and everything to do with people and what it takes to shove them in a better direction.

This better direction may be about leadership, or personal power, or Grace related gifts like healing for man or beast.

Can I ask Dante, about accidents where a horse or a person departs because of it, for instance in a trailer or riding accident?

These were contracts of course, because horse was with man here.

If horse departs from man it was a lesson for the man, which propels him forward to his higher purpose contract within himself.

If man himself died in the accident, with or without horse, it was about a Universal contract that will effect powerful positive change in the end.

Both horse and man always knew their big contract, seemingly hidden at spirit level, if this should happen that someone dies in it.

Nothing is ever empty or pointless, although at the moment you ask why on earth this would happen to such nice people and horses?

It happened because they intended on spirit level an achievement that far outlasts and out-riches the departing experience.

Life is more about play than you know it is, if you could only think about that and grow in that understanding.

It is the levels of the games that had you scratching your head, but now you are getting it more clearly.

What about dying to direct someone?

That happens more than you think or know.

We don't mind and it is always an honour to do so.

You yourself have had this experience, more than once.

This event is always powerfully significant in order to occur to direct a person correctly to their contract.

Would these horses come with a contract to do that with a particular person?

Always a contract for this depth of experience.

How do we thank the horse properly for this?

Not necessary, but always understood.

It is an honour, as I said, for the horse.

No regrets, ever.

Does horse ever die to prevent something for Mankind?

Oh yes.

If horse sees that his biology will out-do his spirit purpose, as in being so dangerous to cause harm, he may choose to depart suddenly.

The person is not yet cognizant of significant imposing harm, but will have had issues where near death thoughts occurred about that horse.

It is rare indeed for horses with advanced contracts, but those with more basic contracts must accede to the safety of the person.

The event will be an accident, a sudden extreme colic, an unexpected event that shakes the person's perception of their relationship.

These decisions are decided very quickly once spirit sees the biology has run away with the horse Being, so to speak.

It is as if biology took over, and spirit could not be heard loudly enough, or consistently enough, to be the primary directive.

These horses are always mighty physically, and always very powerful.

Man will always have recognized their tendency not to listen well, or seeming to be a slow learner in his work.

Trust this horse did not have an advanced contract, as the horse with the advanced contract with you has spirit in the forefront of all action with you, and will never go so far as to cause you to depart.

Some people have been injured with high contracts, but it was part of their personal agreement to be so.

What happens with that horse once he departs? Does he choose a better contract next time?

All participation in life teaches.

This horse grew from the experience, and will be better equipped next time to not be the horse that had trouble learning due to biology.

They don't make this mistake again once they have been through it.

You wonder how horse could let his biology run away with him to this extent, yet people everywhere are laden with this symptom.

Addiction is a classic comparison, where something in your biology takes over and you seem powerless to stop yourself.

When a horse dies, is there a special way to send him on his way?

We go easily without anything special.

We know fully your love for us, and sometimes your indifference to us, but it matters not because it is what God sees at the time in us, which shines brighter than many suns.

Some of us seem lost directly on passing from physical, but quickly receive an inrush of masses of Spirit Beings escorting us, welcoming us, already celebrating for us our return from physical.

If you could help yourself, it would be to see us in celebration and accomplishment, in our finest hour of glory, for that is where we stay until or unless we return.

And can you come back to us when we wish it, or don't know we can wish it?

This is the easiest thing to do, and we often come unwished for.

It was just simpler because prior to this many did not understand we could return.

Now we return in full spirit of course, and as you know sometimes we return as a special blend of more than one horse.

This is a bit of an exception as you can imagine.

If this happens, it was because time for the human would run out for both to return consecutively.

Will there be some physical resemblance anywhere in the returning horse?

More often than not the person will recognize a prominent feature in the returning horse, either in colour, or markings, or behavior.

Always, *always*, the eyes are the key feature that is recognized.

Often the circumstance of finding that returning horse has rather bizarre entry into the human experience, prompting a wondering about why they found that particular horse at that particular time.

Always honour the wondering, as it comes from our connection.

We love this aspect of being horse!

If we saw you were leaving, and asked you to stay, could you?

Not always, but maybe sometimes.

It would take an act of God, so to speak, to affect that.

The purpose of staying would have to far outweigh the desire to leave you.

Such staying purpose is rare indeed, so most of us continue on our chosen path.

But we understand the asking and appreciate the love in it for us.

Does horse always come back as horse?

Of course. Why bother otherwise?

Is it ever so bad that horse does not choose to return?

No. It is only ever so good that we choose not to.

Take for example, your Bethlehem donkey, as you call him.

The contribution to Mankind could never be equalled, and so he had no reason to ever return - has not and will not.

Will a horse stay to help another horse in need?

It has to be dire, and you have seen how a grandmother horse stayed to help the grandson, who could not think about being without female guidance.

This is always rare indeed, but it sometimes is the case.

We will do all we can to prevent you getting sick.

Tell me about vaccinations.

This is a necessary evil of sorts.

We prefer not to get sick if we can help it.

Personally I detest needles, although I accept what you ask me to accept.

Saving a horse life means prolonging the healing relationship, so of course they are worthwhile to do.

What about a lot of vaccines together?

Don't do that if you can avoid it.

Our systems are very powerful, but delicate.

The balance is achieved by staggering vaccines, if possible.

What is the best way to make a needle more tolerable?

Breathe calmly in the giving of it.

Remember to ask for understanding, and explain what is going on.

Some horses relish explanation of all medical procedures, and respond better in the process.

Is there a preferred place?

How do I answer this properly?

Give it in the biggest, strongest muscle mass you can find, and we will give our opinion freely on the degree of placement.

That is, use our butt muscle if possible, but our opinion may involve kicking, so be prepared.

Some horses have died from needles. Were they expressing an idea to Mankind or just ready to leave?

This was a contract higher than the relationship to change it for Horsekind in entirety.

If I were to explain what I needed from a horse, could they choose to comply?

Always.

It depends on the character of the horse and the situation, naturally, but we understand you and to the best of our biology we can comply if we can get all components to agree with our decision.

That is, spirit of us may say, let's help her give me the stomach tube.

Physical may say it is too uncomfortable, so emotions may overreact on behalf of physical and now there is no co-operation.

If physical understands it will be the best it can be, and mental has a relationship with the human, and emotions are soothed in calmness, then compliance is a given.

I give you perfect examples every time you give me needles, which I personally detest.

How important is dentistry to horse now?

When Mankind took over production of our food supply, our teeth had difficulty adjusting.

We no longer had sand to help grind them down and a variety of food to chew on.

So looking after our teeth is now essential for man to do, as we can no longer do it for ourselves.

Look to teeth issues for all kinds of troubles.

Imagine just lifting your head quickly with a toothache, never mind having a bit smack you in a cavity.

Man knows how a bad tooth affects every thought in his head, and we are no different in this category.

Tell me what can happen if your molars are unbalanced.

Unbalanced molars equals unbalanced horse.

Nothing feels connected in a co-ordinated way.

This can be so extreme that our gaits become affected, and taking leads becomes impossible.

It takes a very deep look to assess this.

A proper dental exam is key, as you know.

Hooks, ramps and slanted incisors?

Ouch to all of those.

Particularly where the bit comes in.

This produces nose jerking behaviors as our teeth are clanged against the bit.

Always suspect the teeth.

What's your take on wolf teeth?

These little beggars are seldom an issue, but if they are they are the end-of-the-world type deal for the horse.

So much pain in such a little tooth.

Always check the direction they point as this will determine their degree of involvement in our lives.

Many are just innocent you see.

Tell me why horses grind their teeth.

A most interesting question with many possible reasons.

Sometimes horse is remembering how it helped him think before, like starting the engine of an old Ford.

Grinding the gears so to speak, in forward thought.

Sometimes it is chewing on a situation, literally, making it smaller in horse's estimation in the maceration by his molars.

It is always a contemplative gesture and not an objection gesture as you think it is.

See it as the motor of learning is starting up, and will soon be running more smoothly.

Tell me about worms.

Greedy, little varmints.

A necessary part of give and take and the flow of nature.

Minimize our burdens if you can and we will feel full and rich in our bodies.

What is your opinion of the resistance to some de-wormers?

There comes a time all creatures get a voice, and this creature is saying, "See how strong I am to adapt to your attempts to extinct me."

Yes, that is how worms talk.

Do you have a comment on worming schedules?

Not really.

Depends on the pasture-cruising available to horse.

Small pastures need frequent worm attention, or they run rampant in us.

Why do some horses have allergies?

We are such sensitive individuals, and some of us literally leak our empathy all over the place.

These horses react to all kinds of little energies, and hives are a classic example in a very empathic horse.

Can't be helped - once sensitive always sensitive.

Chronic lameness. What's that about?

Stuck in neutral in Purpose.

The horse feels that he or she is not accomplishing their duty with the person.

The symbology is not moving forward with accomplishment.

What happens then?

There will be interference from outside the situation that changes things up.

Sometimes it is a newcomer with a fresh attitude and outlook.

So sometimes do horses take over for other horses in the same purpose with a person?

Absolutely.

The point is the contract for growth and expansion was set and will be fulfilled by one or another.

How does the first horse feel about not accomplishing the contract with the person?

Never badly.

We are all together in general purpose and sharing is to be expected.

We never feel bad in spirit. It is not possible.

What does the first horse do when a second comes in to finish the purpose with the person?

Often that horse moves on to new purpose elsewhere that is more suitable athletically.

Sometimes the horse is retired, or disposed of in another manner.

Oh.

Does every horse come with a distinct purpose?

Yes, but not all of the same intensity.

Some have delightful light purpose, and some have deep intense purpose, but they all come with purpose.

Some horses have general plans to be of general help, and some come bound to one person with divine intention to change the world.

There was a very famous horse with a very serious injury a few years ago, and he had potential to excel here powerfully. What happens in a situation like that, where everything is done to help but the horse does not make it?

It turned out that the impact of his illness and death achieved higher notoriety than what he could have achieved on the physical level.

Eyes were opened that were stubbornly shut and many, many hearts were won in this horse's public medical battle.

Highest purpose was through the injury and support he received nationwide.

He literally melted hearts with his story.

Always assess where the highest demonstration of magnificent feeling is present, and there you find the answer to why did this happen like that?

More people became conscious with kindness, generosity, and love toward animals because of this horse's story.

Chronic lung disease. What's that about?

Sometimes horses encounter situations that restrict full spirit expression.

Our spiritual chest, so to speak, becomes tight.

This is generally a part of the journey for us, secretly setting us up for success at the later stages.

We endure the little discomforts that prepare us fully for later expansion.

Me, for example - I have small airway disease.

It represented my early venture into an unhappy circumstance, where I was ignored and forgotten, and my purpose seemed dead.

When you came, I began the recovery in breathing in spirit, but retained the physical scars reminding me of my sacrifice in my early spirit adventures.

It is really insignificant to me, and only serves as a reminder of my degree of devotion to my contract, to endure whatever came, until you came.

So, let's talk about some injuries. Bruises and foot abscesses – is that a particular kind of comment to people?

Of course.

A small objection perhaps to work, or the farrier.

It says look to my feet and what happens there, something is amiss.

It may also say, with experience, I just don't feel like work now, and know I will get a break with a simple abscess.

Tell me about the farrier part.

Some farriers are adept, and some are not.

Especially if the farrier dislikes his experience with the horse, we may offer this kind of objection.

He will consider what he did the next time when you inform him or he notices we had an abscess.

He may do a more thorough job, or he may, if he is searching for meaning in life, so to speak, think that there was something about himself that did something in the horse's foot.

There are many farriers constantly appraising their performance, and assessing their input to foot problems.

Tell your farrier, and something will catch fire in him to approach the foot with concern, which may be all it takes to address the abscess-prone-choice for the horse.

We like it when the farrier shows he cares.

Very, very simple.

What can speed up the healing here?

Acceptance and appreciation for the process.

Try for the answer by examining the work the horse is in and his relative happiness, or his happiness with the farrier.

How bad does an abscess hurt?

It's tolerable, just ouchy for the most part.

Not agonal or we wouldn't choose it so lightly.

What can help physically?

Nothing really.

It has its own mind per se and works its way through the steps from beginning to end methodically.

Rarely can digging enhance the process as it is already up in tissues where it does not belong.

Soaking the abscess?

This makes the person feel better about it, but the soaking does not get deep enough to bring it to a head.

Once it drains, go ahead and soak.

We do appreciate the attention, regardless, so if you feel like soaking and spending time with us that is fine with us.

I cringe to see you limping.

Yes, we expect that.

Does the comment ever reflect something else?

So you get the message loud and clear now.

We will pester you until you understand our message here, and we appreciate your understanding this morning.

We will also object in this manner if the discrepancy in energies between handlers and human partners screams loudly at us.

Once horse has experienced the wholeness of man, we will not tolerate lesser energies well, if at all.

All horses have difficulty in their knowing excellent energy and then trying to withstand less positive energy.

See the brilliant horses that won't do what the amateur asks - they only want the best of riders and horsemen now.

This is evident everywhere.

Sometimes it might be better for Horsekind not to have known the excellence of Humankind, for our objection under saddle is often mistaken for non-responsiveness when we are trying our guts out to withstand how you are asking something of us in a short-of-excellence way.

Pretend you knew the best, and now you know the worst.

How long could your heart endure that?

So we may ask for a new foot caregiver in this way, with chronic abscessation.

You will recognise unhappiness with our performance easily related to foot care, and you will wonder at the farrier's competence, but it is often our comment on your excellence in energy with us, and lack of it in them.

The best farrier may make us a perfect foot, but do it begrudgingly; an abscess gets everyone thinking how to prevent the next one.

Technique is less important than benevolent energy towards horse, for a lightness of energy makes a happier foot.

Is every horse this susceptible when inspired to object?

Of course.

We all get a voice here.

Some wait a bit longer if they are able to endure due to character, and some do not withstand a hint of disparity and the result is immediate disease.

Laminitis – it seems certain horses are prone to it. Is there a particular reason?

This experience relates to multiple opinions regarding purpose.

It is a deep-seated opinion to be so effective and sometimes has long lasting effects that reflect this depth.

Relate it to something like diabetes, where energy related sources are mismanaged.

In these horses, this is evident.

The horse has not directed his energies as appropriately as possible, getting distracted from his story with his person, and this halts the detour effectively.

He has an opinion and Source has an opinion that have momentarily differed.

"Wake up", says Source, "you're on the wrong road!"

And this is how it is stopped, in his feet.

Horse literally cannot move forward in the wrong direction.

Some horses wrestle with the effects of founder many years, or much of their life.

It does not have to be so dramatic.

Resolve the issue that God stopped horse in and you are off and running again.

So how does a horse get off track?

We start thinking of other things that are right under our noses, instead of keeping our focus on the big picture.

Easy to do and most of Mankind lives like this.

Can you give me an example of how a horse could get off track?

Of course I can.

Imagine I am training for the Iditarod race, but I am fascinated by food.

All I care about is who is getting my share of the food supply, and I mistakenly eat too much for one dog.

We are talking about a dog here then?

Yes. It is simpler to explain.

So now the dog gets fat, and incapable of running his race that he came to glorify in, in this lifetime.

He never meant to eat so much, he just got lost in his biology momentarily, and now he is replaced by another dog that was more suitable for the race.

See how horse could think food was more significant than waiting for his moment with his person, when he would have the opportunity to express fully his purpose with them, be it a gentle time together, or a working moment displaying working purpose.

Should he focus intently on eating, it is so good you see, that fresh green grass, and biology swings him away from purpose, now he will have no choice but to notice it in his feet.

I know you are thinking there must be something more relevant I could use, but it is really a perfect example.

Thank-you for that.

Is it because he has strayed from purpose that the biology now surfaces more powerfully, as if spirit got put on the back burner for the time being?

Yes, and yes, you got that from me.

Sometimes you answer before I finish the asking.

Generally always.

Will we figure out the issue on our own, about you diminished in spirit purpose and stuck in biology?

Of course, for the most part.

It may be about depth of care, or suitability for the human.

The horse got seriously distracted in purpose to meet this trauma in the first place.

The horse is able to refocus but if he gets off track again, the issue will re-surface.

Always examine the spiritual issue first; it always has a spirit base.

Some breeds seem more prone to laminitis, and crest-y horses as a rule. Why is that?

These horses are tied strongly to purpose, so more likely to be stopped when off track.

Also, they were very popular due to magnificence, so had opportunity to bond with Mankind by the thousands and thousands.

When a type of horse has this impact on Mankind, you can bet he is so, so sensitive and bound to powerful purpose, and so God is watching very, very closely.

Should he waiver from this exceptional purpose with such opportunity for change in so many, many people, God will be sure to pay attention.

So these beautiful, powerful necked horses are sure to be stopped if they waiver from their purpose.

Count on it.

Man explains this as insulin resistance.

He would have to find a biological excuse, yes.

But trust that is the tip of the iceberg.

The way God corrects them is set up ahead of time, and the biology has to agree with God's intention for those horses.

Tell me about the disease we call Cushing's.

This manifestation is about the use of fight and flight throughout the life of that particular horse.

He has likely endured significant trauma at some point that has made him ever watchful and over-reactive in order not to endure such a situation again.

He in fact had an opportunity to return to spirit but decided to stay and give it another go, so to speak, and his biology had to re-vamp to comply.

He now has more than enough hormone to run three lifetimes from the bear, or the experience that induced his thoughts more to leaving.

Trust that at some point in these horses' lives, they lived more than they chose to due to circumstance of ownership, and overrode the call home to be of further service in this lifetime, but adapted medically to the surplus side of hormone to do so.

This disease is of little bother to horse, having served him so well in his requirement for surplus readiness to flee, or stand and fight, although how horse sometimes stands and fights, does not look like it to Mankind.

Do bad backs have particular significance?

This horse carried a spiritual burden of magnanimous proportion, as if he came already weakened due to choice of contract.

The presentation of the disease always has an interesting reflective quality to the path of the horse this lifetime.

Know horse had choice in what he came to bear, and did it willingly.

See the horse with a dipped back as a timeless reminder of what horse has carried for Mankind for centuries.

Chronic arthritis in knees, ankles, stifles…

All about how horse was objecting to his forward direction.

Notice how horses with big knees and other joints just cope with it, sail along in the pasture with it, don't speak of it or complain of it by refusal to participate.

Consider all we experienced to exhibit visually this enlargement of our powerhouse particulars.

All a part of our life story.

Never think for one moment that we consider ourselves crippled by it, or inhibited in any way, even though to you we look like we are hobbling around.

We hold in our perception of our physical selves, the specifics of wellness, and magnificent carriage of body and limbs, and see for the most part how we were before the thing came that you concentrate on with us.

Horse has the ability to see himself whole in his former glory.

Sometimes when you speak with horse, he won't mention the thing you most want to know about, because for him it is non-existent and so insignificant to his real story.

Tell me about nose bleeds.

An exclamation mark to that point in the story.

"So done with that experience", horse says. "Never again."

Now what was the experience you ask, that made horse stop in his tracks and bleed all over the place?

It was the perception that no matter what he would be thrust forward in the wrong direction for his contracts.

"You are doing this no matter what," man says, and horse replies, "Notice my weakness here. I am unsuitable. Pick somebody else in order for me to find my deepest contract."

See this horse as a spokesperson for the industry specifically, and note that in spite of his apparent suitability for the event he is participating in, he has powerful druthers and a way to speak them that has you searching for a solution.

Most bleeders bleed for the choice of earth occupation.

Sometimes the odd event is enough to induce a degree of consideration and care that pleases and soothes horse in the participation of the wayward, so to speak, occupation to him.

It may then resolve itself, giving more depth for horse to delve into if this surfaces as a result of his exclamation mark.

Or, if he sees clearly the only way to accomplish his most heart driven desire is with another person, he will continue to have nose bleeds, and be moved in the direction of his heart due to insecurity in his performance.

Tell me about blood disorders, like low-grade anemia.

A subtle expression of dislike in occupation.

It will manifest as lack of endurance within the thing that man has chosen for the horse.

It will resist cure and cause man to contemplate the nature of the cause of the blood problem, and he will wrestle within himself in misunderstanding.

Eventually the condition will exacerbate into non-performance if the person cannot get it through his head that the horse is saying "no, not my thing", gently.

See these horses as gentle guides in the beginning of initiation into the spirit science relationship of disease.

It always troubles Mankind, and always means something important.

We don't need more iron; we need more understanding of what we are more suited to be doing in earth work.

What about navicular disease?

This also represents stuck-ness in purpose.

It could be purpose with horse, or purpose within the person.

So you need to examine your own journey if your horse has symptoms of navicular.

It is compounded by difficulty in comprehension of whose path it is about.

But generally look to the person's path with this disease.

So horse may have something going on in his feet that has nothing to do with him but is representational of his person's life in some way?

Yes, some things only.

Navicular is a degenerative disease so what is the symbology here?

Perfect description of the breakdown of communication in the person's life, with someone prominent in their life path.

How else would it be demonstrated better?

Are you telling me this is really not about the horse at all?

Yes. Truly.

I would feel really badly if I knew I was to blame for this in my horse.

How else would we demonstrate this to you if we are not willing to undergo some discomfort that gets you thinking and talking?

You begin to talk with others who have been through it with their horse, you begin to research the best way to help our feet, you explore veterinary cures, you explore better footwear for us, and you begin to communicate with purpose now, not so distracted by the colour of your hair that week.

You begin to *be* purposeful now, because this is an important disease for horse, and you are the one who has to find the answers for our cure.

Communication gets a serious, grounded base for you and this helps you in your life purpose too.

Yes, navicular is our way of yelling at you with our biology, because of the negativity in the horse world about it.

Get moving, get thinking, get caring, get busy communicating with the right channels; it is time to grow like never before!

Is this kind of demonstration regarding the person, in the horse, applicable to only certain horse character types?

Yes, the deep contracts will have deep-seated damage demonstrated in horse.

This is worrisome.

Don't worry about it, just recognize it.

This is key to recovery, and recovery is truly possible always in spirit driven demonstrations.

This represents a new aspect to diseases for you, I know.

How fascinating to know there is a reason for it that you can find and resolve, and voila, your horse recovers regardless of treatment.

Look to your inward self with navicular, heart and spavin.

These represent communication breakdown, love and heartbreak, and wrong occupation.

Look to your lives and ask what you are involved in that communication would help, what relationship is it that needs attention, or is it time to move on from your present work.

Spavin represents grinding your heels away without purpose.

Change it up when your horse shows up with these three things.

Back to laminitis for a moment, is that always horse stuck and not human?

Yes. This is *our* warning, degeneration of the thing that holds us together symbolically.

Hoof wall to foot, purpose to spirit.

So how might we practically help this horse that is stuck in purpose when we may not have any idea of his real purpose in our relationship?

Such an excellent question.

If you have a horse with laminitis, acute or chronic, you know now it is purpose related.

The horse cannot go forward in the direction he was going in his working life.

If he was a pasture horse, he needs a working relationship.

If he was a working horse, he needs his earth work changed up.

If he has shown any indication during your earth horse work, like loving the trail over the jump, or loving to jump over cutting the cow, see that as your sign of what his purpose is related to.

So many horses get picked for the human's idea of what they want to do with them, but we have our own ideas of what we love to do with our bodies.

If we get placed in a working environment that is not to our real honest liking for our body and purpose, we will revolt in our feet.

It cannot be otherwise to make you pay attention to our dismay in our earth work that does not permit our true full radiance in purpose.

Of course we have physical purpose that enhances our spirit purpose.

Why else would the magnificent Arabian come beautiful if he did not wish to attract those to whom beauty is mostly skin deep, and now the real work begins to see beauty in heart too?

So physical things are linked to spiritual things to affect a result in contract purpose.

I have strayed from topic on purpose to enhance your understanding about why a lovely, chubby trail horse who longs to do dressage, will founder.

Not my full expression of purpose he says.

I need more to be all I came to be.

This may distress the soul who wants him to be a trail horse, but it will change it up sufficiently so that he may be parted with to meet his big contract, or will be sold as a garbage horse to someone with a heart contract so huge he is able to recover fully, and be complete as trail horse because of the heart contract.

Look at the physical and see if horse is happy in occupation.

This will be clear in your mind when you ask that question.

Ideas will come to you that you will doubt are true, until they come again and again out of the blue of thought, and now you realize, this must be coming from your horse.

So now you have an idea of what makes us happy.

Can you adjust our working position with you to include that or not?

If you cannot change the work we do here in earth school with you, consider is there someone that will be able to take us from you and use us in another capacity that may be more suitable.

This situation with another person will appear if it is meant to be.

If you do not find another situation for us, and we seem completely useless to you, the answer will come that we need to go from you back to spirit for renewal.

You will be rocked with guilt perhaps at this idea, which will promote further searching for an alternative, and generally in this deep searching you will grow towards your purpose, satisfying at least part of our contract.

We never mind all of this thinking commotion that we create when we are stuck.

It is all tied to growth in some manner.

If you can keep us, recognizing this horse needs something to feel back on track, more useful and on purpose, then we will heal profoundly and quickly from this, because hope has been added to our medication.

You will understand this better as it soaks in you.

Don't fret about it.

We don't.

I love that hope is medication. And how a heart contract could change the horse's situation enough that a previous occupation that he was unhappy in, he is now happy in. Got it.

And everything else but those three (navicular, heart and spavin), look to the horse's path as creating the thing we see?

That is correct.

And what about treating those things?

Of course we appreciate corrective shoeing, medication and appropriate medical attention, and it all helps us correct the physical issue.

But the true healing, the healing that gives longevity to horse that has shown these diseases, is dependent on the spirit purpose being corrected - so always, now that you know, search for what might need changing up spirit-wise.

And heart?

These issues seldom can be corrected, but within the horse compensation grows for it, and surprisingly, these horses do extremely well as long as the issue that they reflected can be addressed.

It may be addressed by the person, or sometimes, it is addressed by God for them.

It is like your angels say, enough of that now, get cracking, and change this up now.

And yes, the angels help horse in this too.

We are never alone in our purpose with you, and God sees the troubled heart of horse and helps, always.

A heart murmur Dante. Would God soothe it?

Oh yes.

Especially once horse was re-directed to a heart contract with affection, now horse has everything to make his heart sing for many years.

So this might involve horse finding a new person then.

Generally this is the case.

I understand that horse can help man with emotions, for example sadness over a broken heart. If horse can help, and tends to be able to not absorb emotions for himself, why then do some horses get a heart medical issue?

These horses had this contract - very simple.

As a rule horses have most excellent hearts and it is truly rare to have a problem.

It is not to say that our heart will not ache for you in some contracts, but most horses simply have a deep knowing of your emotion and are able to act indifferently but still love you deeply.

It is like the example when a person goes to a Counsellor person, and weeps continuously.

If the Counsellor also weeps continuously, no one is helped.

One person must hold the emotional space for the other to be free to release the emotion themselves.

Horse holds the emotional space for you, has a workable plan to take the emotion for you, and ends up empowering you in the process.

If we wept with you, we would be no use to you.

It does not mean we do not love you deeply, just because we do not weep.

So trust if heart becomes an issue, you had this contract for powerful teaching in yourself because of what your horse took on.

The teaching will become clear to you, as it is your path, and not ours.

And the horses that die suddenly of heart related things?

These horses came with great intention to speak a message to Mankind about heart.

If they die young from heart, they have grabbed your heart as a rule, and initiated something grander in it than you imagined could be in human heart.

They have enacted a physical change in heart depth of perception, so to speak, and now the human that interacted with that horse being has been helped powerfully into the next level of their spiritual adventure.

It is never done without great purpose in mind, this sudden dying of a creature noted for steady and powerful heart.

To accept this that goes against nature of horse, it must be only for powerful growth related to heart in a person.

That person's heart is likely to already be huge in horse estimation and horse agrees to an uncommonly grander purpose in an already exceptional heart, for it to be eased into greater spiritual heart depth.

And yes, they had a contract for it, you better believe it on this one!

I think I finally get it about heart! This one was hard to get my mind around.

Yes, when we are known for such excellent hearts, and so many people have in their words, broken hearts, so why doesn't every horse have one?

It is a rare and powerful contract, it's that simple.

To summarize, if you are with a horse that has a heart issue it is one of two things.

Either you have a contract where the horse will physically accept your heartache in the form of heart disease, thus lessening your heartache for you, or if the horse dies of heart related issues, he has a contract with you to launch your already magnificent heart onto another plain of heart depth that was inaccessible to you before your involvement with him.

Now you have it fully.

And spavin, the third thing horse will physically demonstrate that is really from us?

This person is stuck in dreadful occupation that is stifling their contract growth in all areas of their lives.

You see the image of someone scraping their heels trying to escape something as they go backwards on their bottom.

That is what we perceive, and what we are reflecting in our own heels.

This contract to take on the demonstration reflecting occupational dismay is also fairly uncommon.

If you have a horse with spavin, examine your occupation happiness, for spavin is the visual, physical thing exhibiting your screams to do something you love.

And yes, we can adapt and heal fairly well from spavin, but the true lasting healing comes best when man gets this.

When horse takes on a physical demonstration in himself because of what his person endures, and this is specifically in their contract, the act of taking it on changes the energy in the thing that despaired the person.

It is impossible to describe to you how that happens at this time, but trust that our magnificent bodies are in truth such powerful energy changers for you, and we are capable of mutating the negativity about your life circumstance through our physical demonstration.

When we mutate, so to speak, your sadness, or worry, or fear about your life stuff, this does not require the aid of our physical.

This is the purest way to explain it.

Emotion is so easy for horse to help you with as a rule, but if we need to enlist the power and the largeness of our physical being to beef up the grabbing in our spiritual fists your dealings with communication, heartbreak and dreadful occupation – three very BIG aspects of being human - then we enlist, literally, foot, heart and hocks, our powerhouses of physical, to do this.

Do not worry yourselves about our generosity here.

It is horse at his best, and our full intention to participate in our contracts with you.

I have certainly had all three of those troubles, yet you never developed those diseases.

Not our contract of course.

The understanding you have given me here, is that because you have moved those energies for us, it has opened up the space for other helpful energies from outside of horse that will flow to us now in those areas in communication, heartbreak and occupation. So we don't have to worry that we struggle in some emptiness to figure stuff out, the Universe will then flow the help to us that we need because of the energy you were able to change for us.

Brilliant.

Tell me about uveitis. It has plagued us in our understanding of it.

Horse can't look at something.

Horse has seen what he didn't want to see, been exposed to something too difficult to look at, and decided not to.

This disease is pure spirit based.

The reason man can't figure out the cause of this disease is that very thing.

All kinds of little culprits have been indicated, and are found vaguely floating within horse from time to time, but they are not the cause.

Horse just can't look anymore.

The thing may be an idea - an understanding of cruelty, neglect, or harshness met by souls of such gentle nature they would rather lose an eye than see it.

Trust this thing is about seeing something undesirable that created thought that horse preferred not to think about.

We feel completely at ease choosing this, as the good it does far outweighs the bother the blind eye is to us.

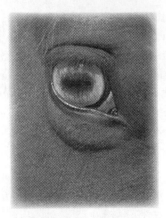

Can this be helped or cured?

Not cured.

But remove us from the thing if you can recognize it, see for us what we can't look at, and change what you can think about changing.

We used to blame the moon.

Yes, comical that.

All moon ever does is for good, not evil.

How do we see for you what you can't look at?

This thing that started the reaction in eye needs to be noticed by Mankind.

See it for its mistaken take on life, its wrongful idea of things, and its sad excuse for reality.

Say to it in your mind and heart, "I see you there, cruelty, or sadness, or barbaric practice, but for my horse, I will see you through the eyes of God, knowing you are but asleep in spirit for now, doing the best you can from your sleepy position in the world."

Wow.

So when it returns in horse, this uveitis, have they seen or remembered the thing they couldn't look at?

They began to get lost in it again.

Our excellent memories don't help this disease.

Like crying over something sad when you remember it.

The eye overreacts in memory and you call this a flare-up.

It is memory, not moon, which causes the recurrence.

Are these horses particularly sensitive in some aspect of horse character for eyes to be affected?

Of course.

Visionary horses for the most part, able to maintain full perception of the good in Mankind, despite the vision before them.

Blocking is an option to minimize distraction that would pretend life was otherwise.

Life is not that thing before them and they won't look.

No more, it says.

Stop showing me something you made up to tease me into thinking it is real life.

I know only the real story, and all is well at my core. Fibber!

How does horse cope with one blind eye, or both?

We see in ways you can't imagine.

Earth helps, wind helps, and other horses help.

We feel everything through our feet, and have a knowing of general things instantly.

Our hearing is so exceptional to begin with, and it serves us profoundly when we can't see.

Yes, we feel sound too.

Take it gently if we can't see well for riding.

Trail is fine, but performance is obviously out of the question.

Let us do it in our own time, and we can still astound you.

People feel blind horses are not trustworthy on the blind side.

That makes sense to think we are less reliable there, but we have a knowing of what is around us in feeling energy coming toward us, or leaving - like breathing in and out.

Earth and trees and hills and rocks - all move energy that we perceive.

People have this ability; it is just asleep for most.

Trust that we are capable beings.

Trust that we would think before running into something we can't see.

Always expect horse has more sources of information to rely on that you can't perceive.

We read it all.

That's why blind horses do so well.

And we remember every little rock in the pasture.

In new places we need introduction, but use your good sense in our housing situation, and we will be very, very safe.

I have heard heart warming stories about horses being guide horses.

It is just like mother and foal.

It is easy to sense the presence of another horse and follow it, and the guide knows exactly what has happened to the blind horse.

We communicate completely with each other, knowing our infirmities, and are able to rise to the occasion and assist when necessary.

Is there an adjustment period as a horse's vision diminishes?

The more gradual the better we adapt, as we become used to not seeing and adjust.

Sudden loss of vision takes a dramatic adaptation, and we appreciate teaching from man in this situation.

Best case scenario is to give us a buddy horse for earthly eyes.

Does growing older change a horse's normal vision?

Not much.

Some horses tend to fade certain things out of their vision, literally, preferring a smaller focus area as age permits.

These horses have seen a lot in their time, and the eyes now rest from identifying work for them, so to speak.

Night can be most trying to navigate once the eyes mute their focus somewhat.

But we compensate reasonably.

You may see this change as dullness in our pupil, but it is not blindness to all things, we just narrowed our field of concern with our focus.

There was a very famous horse that went blind which was timed with an injection of an antibiotic. Yet he continued to work and perform to the amazement of all who watched him. How did he see?

He had reached the place of oneness with his human, and literally saw through his human's eyes what the human was looking at when they worked together.

The human had to maintain excellent focus, and send excellent pictures in thought to the horse, and he had the ability to do this based on their lifetime together doing it when he was a seeing horse.

It made very little difference to this horse and he adapted quickly.

This is what can be achieved in pictures and is a perfect example of the co-operative dance between trainer and horse.

Not all achieve this, but it is something to strive for and remember it is possible.

Just for fun Dante, tell me about head shaking.

This is about misunderstanding the connection between purpose and path.

The horse has literally lost track of the way, and is scrambling for a way to re-establish this connection.

See it as literal as people, who look at something and shake their head at it in bewilderment.

Such is this behavior, rooted in lost-ness of the way to powerful purpose.

There was a major distraction to be so misled, and finding the source of that is the answer to correcting the demonstration.

The distraction is often a seemingly sudden re-routing of the physical horse from owner to owner or place to place, and the horse has not been able to establish the spirit direction fast enough before being moved away again.

It is like a foster children situation, going from foster home to foster home, but never finding a mom and dad.

These horses are searching for their contracts with their people, and not coping with the interval which contains so much commotion.

Do you know what fixes it?

Permanency of situation.

This horse must sense solidly the attachment of the owner and the stability of the environment.

Longevity in situation allows the behavior to diminish for the most part.

There will come a time when horse is convinced he has found what he thought he had lost, and the behavior becomes bothersome to him as well, and he weans himself of it.

And cribbing?

Boredom with our story and needed something to read.

The wood creates a connection to earth for us that centers us and relieves our mental placement at that time.

If you have a cribbing horse, change his story for him, and make life interesting.

And wind sucking?

These horses are inwardly screaming.

Horse can't scream outward, and if you look at how this behavior appears, the air is simply going in the other direction so forcefully, so intently, and so powerfully as to exact a scream from life itself.

It is a rough, uncomfortable thing to watch, even for horse.

What happened in this horse's life to create a screaming consistent behavior that becomes an addiction so overwhelming that control seems impossible?

Trust that these individuals are part of an endurance program embedded deep in horse society, and they are designated in their point of industry to speak for horse.

Look to the breed mostly to identify the issue that needs to be screamed and let go of.

Trust that the designated screamer speaks for many horses in his action, and try to solve the issue for him by creating the most peaceful horse existence possible in the situation.

If horse can remember the Truth here, that all is well at its base, then he can stop this behavior so annoying to himself, for he dislikes being responsible for the designated screaming, that is so repulsive to both horse and Mankind.

It is a last ditch effort, if horse has to scream at his or another's circumstance.

Perhaps the best and surest cure is to take horse aside and say, "I understand why you scream for your situation, and for others who cannot scream themselves. I will scream with you in my own way, so you are not alone. I recognize you endure repulsion and disgust from Mankind for this behavior, but now I understand, and I appreciate you for your position in this, and for your ability to withstand our disgust, for I know it is difficult to endure the compounded negativity of the situation you scream at, and the negativity of man as he sees you scream. So scream, dear Horse, and let me help you by supporting your important release of what would otherwise cause you to lose your mind."

Then see what your acceptance and support of the behavior brings in a little time, because changing the circumstance is not always possible.

Acceptance is key for the horse in this role.

More for us here?

We never, not one of us, wishes to be ill or damaged.

If we can find a way to show you and teach you without disintegrating in our biology, we will do that.

If the extreme is required to demonstrate to you the significance of our purpose with you, for your purpose, we will gladly take it on with no condemnation of the circumstance that required it.

Such is horse, and such is the importance of horse contracts with man.

At least try to think about our injury, and if a nagging idea persistently appears about the event in us, know it is a spirit thing that you should explore in you, and secondly, in us.

Always think it is about you first, because body is a voice for us when it is all we've got.

If you can see that we horse-onally, have been removed from significant purpose and you identify it, then look to *us* for a reflection of disparity in our purpose.

We will need a change of venue to support us in purpose if you see us with chronic disease that seemingly defies explanation or treatment.

This chronic aspect of failure in our biology is always horse.

So knowing this chronic demonstration is us, change something for us in environment, trainer, farrier, veterinarian or rider.

We are telling you as loud as silence permits that we are stuck in purpose and something has to go.

We will send you an idea that keeps popping up in your mind about what we need, and you will think it is yours, to which we say, "Hoorah - who cares - just help me move from here!"

Do not worry that it won't come to you; just remember my words and it will be like an electric shock to your brain.

"I bet it's that!" You will say, and you will be right.

You are not left helpless to figure out the thing that plagues us - never lose sleep over that.

Above all, know that spirit will use biology to talk to you about what we need to happen to be helped.

And we so understand this *is* your desire, to help us.

It is never a one-way deal, this thing with horse and man.

We would never have committed to you if that were so.

Rest with these ideas now, and they will resonate and blossom when needed.

Chapter Twelve
Emotion-Biology-Mind

So I see this big, practical, opinionated horse before me, yet you are so much when it comes to emotions. Tell me about horse emotions.

Well…you know we take your stuff for you, asked or unasked.

We must be able to not take it so personally as to endure it ourselves, so your emotions are yours, and we see them rather indifferently because we must.

Our own emotions are different, because they are linked to our biology so tightly.

For example, I look crabby when I correct a colt that is in my space.

Necessary posture, yet I am not crabby.

I am able to correct without being mad.

I am able to discipline with fairness and expectancy from the other horse.

So discipline is unemotional for me and the other horse.

We suffer not emotionally, using emotions as mere indicators of something to assess in biology or mental aspects.

We sort of chew on what happened, sometimes literally, as we process the message the emotion brought us.

Emotion is a flag to us - "Oh, look, my biology is making me think I should leave this area now."

Am I afraid? No, processing the emotion that warned me of danger.

To humans we look afraid, but we are biologically programmed to add emotion in that situation, and now we need to read the situation the emotion told us about.

What about horses we see shaking and dripping sweat from a "fearful" event?

These guys tripped a big emotional trigger that overwhelmed thinking processes, and so much biology happened that it is difficult to catch up.

But it will catch up.

The bigger the flag the more biology we are dealing with.

Nobody wants to be eaten by the lion, and many use this analogy for us in training.

But the facts are we are using emotion as the warning flag, and the bigger the event that hits our biology the bigger our biology reacts, so shaking and sweating are demonstrated in the extreme.

But trust that spirit will wrestle with biology and we will process the thing that loomed as perceived danger.

In the meantime, a quiet word of encouragement will be the most reassuring thing you can gift us in that moment.

Don't hang on to us for dear life in the event of the big emotional flagging - just get out of the way and trust we will get it together according to our ability to participate in the big picture.

Bigger contracts - bigger picture.

Bigger contracts - bigger reaction to the emotion flag.

When you get a horse with which you have this bigger contract, expect your learning curve to be huge to match.

Our emotions we demonstrate also help you adapt to the same emotion in yourselves.

The mirror imagery is very useful here.

If you are afraid in life, we will make you deal with our being afraid in life.

You will struggle to find confidence for us, and instill it in yourselves in the process.

Am I going too fast?

Not sure. Let me summarize about fear. You look afraid sometimes. And some horses seem so justified in the perception of fear. Help me with that.

Fear comes on many levels of distraction.

The physical biology deals with it first and deepest.

Yes, we run from the lion, and the rope if we are wild.

Self-preservation will always overrule mental in the moment.

So expect us to demonstrate "we are so out of here!" in cases where we perceive physical danger, being loss of a limb, or even mind.

On the mental level, we are thinking very quickly how deep the perceived danger is.

Will it overcome my biology or not?

The mind moves quickly, but the biology of the horse moves faster and first.

So body first, and then mind is catching up.

Emotion is the thing that rallies all but spirit level.

When horse is emotional, which you generally perceive as fear, emotion is setting it all in motion per se, whether we move or not at that time.

Some of us can freeze in fear when the situation is one of losing one's mind, not one's limbs.

These horses are crying out for help with conditioning their biology.

See these horses explode and injure self and person if close to them.

Mind is always more precious to lose than limb, although you may be startled to hear that.

Trust it is so.

Are there times when the spirit part of horse can overcome the emotion we call fear?

Oh yes.

This is demonstrated every day all over the world.

In big contracts, we are able to control reactions in biology better, especially once the main parts of the contract are moving forward well.

Now this is where you see amazing moments that you never thought you'd see.

For instance, although I still remember my tendency to buck when objecting to your fear on the trail, now, conditioned or not to buck, I don't.

Your fear fed my fear, but now our spirit growth together changed all that.

So we call it fear, but that is not correct is it?

No. The term we use is flight ready.

All is positive energy in horse and fear has a negative energy connotation, so incorrect terminology for horse.

There is no negative in the Being horse.

Do us a favour; change your description for us to flight ready.

See the energy scale in the positive, from complacent, safe, quiet, peace energy to high-powered flight response capable of zooming us out of negative energy zones to a better energy match.

It is only positive energy in horse.

It is only ever the situation we are in that brings negative onto the scene.

It is only positive energy at the base of Mankind as well, but you have trouble seeing it clearly in yourselves.

We will see it for you when you can't.

This is an integral part of horse, seeing the best of you before us, in spite of the presentation energy.

It is quite simple to think about if you know we seek the high energy best match in the moment, and flee from the negative energy that is grating on our nerves, so to speak.

Thank-you for that understanding, it makes great sense to me.

So your contract with me had you bucking with me. Would you buck with another person?

First of all there was no way I could end up with another person, but if you loaned me out to ride, no, I wouldn't bother as I do not have anything big going on with them.

So what we call fear is a process of emotion waking up your biology first, then you begin to process it mentally, and once that is underway and the thing is dealt with mentally, then the biology calms down.

Yes, you have it.

So the next time you meet the same thing, what happens?

We always grow from a situation that evokes emotion, so the next time we will have an understanding of consequences.

If the thing is still huge in mind, as mind has considered it and believes it a plausible reason to leave the area, we will still leave the area.

If mind has examined it fully and determined otherwise, now we can stand and observe, reserving leaving only if something unexpected raises its head in the situation.

To teach us to handle our biology better, let us participate briefly, then exit.

We now have a reasonable expectation of co-operation with the thing that evoked the passion of flight before in us.

Passion may be a better word than fear for us, as emotion has levels of depth that either tell us it is mild or extreme.

Passion is on the high end, and fear has such a negative connotation, when really it is high emotion setting things rolling.

We have come full term with this now.

Do horses ever get mad at their people?

You would think we might, but no, that is not our style.

We may get very firm, but never mad.

Now firm to a horse is pretty firm, so our demonstrations might look like we have a temper, but we just had to get really big to get your attention.

What about frustrated?

This goes way deeper than that word.

We get soul-sick, some of us.

Such a horse will shut down expression of being.

We are still present and fully spirit present, but the rest of us demonstrates exhaustion of biology, mind and emotion.

Such demonstration can be the result of these endless circles; why be present in such situations?

Some result from inept consciousness of Mankind.

Very simple to recognize this emotion in horse.

Now, what can you do to help this horse?

Just be. Just be present.

Don't hug us as we cannot endure that discrepancy in energy between a hug and despair in soul.

But be with us in quiet consideration of all we have endured.

That is all we need to be better.

Sit, sing, and sweep the floor.

Be with us.

There will come a time you see in our eyes a change.

You will see in our gait a jig.

Now spirit is recovering and beginning to party with biology.

Go quietly now, no surprises.

And we will become whole again.

Do horses feel or have jealousy?

We look like it sometimes, but it is really about boss mare stuff and all dominance linked behavior.

It's just, don't mess with my stuff, or eat my grain, or stand in my spot under the tree.

All about what goes with being the horse boss, and so on down the line.

What about regret?

Yes, we harbour this briefly from time to time.

Always about contracts and our part in them if we stray off-line.

It never lasts, and it never overwhelms us, as we have mechanisms to cope and protect ourselves from spirit level.

God would never allow horse to steep in regret; it is too against our nature and purpose with you.

Worry?

It appears to be part of us, but don't think for a moment that we dwell on what is coming at us tomorrow.

What is coming this moment has a no-time-to-worry aspect.

I may look like I am worried, but I am assessing the situation, and determining in my biology what should be done or will be required.

We think too fast to worry, but our biology dealing with the moment may look like we dwell on a topic when we are dispersing biology reactions.

Tell me about your sense of humour.

Vast, limitless, and a true expression of horse in the moment.

We love to play, with or without you.

Give us free range and a sunny day and the world is our playground.

The blades of grass sing a chorus to us and the ground welcomes our hoof prints.

Add wind in our tails and there is glory for you.

Do horses smile and laugh?

Many smile, but not as you know it.

It is mostly in our eyes and actions of our mouths.

Sometimes it is evident in our style of posture and the way we toss our hair.

As for laughing, it is only our heart that has this capacity.

And laugh we do, at our circumstance or plight, for sometimes it is all a horse can do.

However, we love to make you laugh.

It is one of our greatest delights and precious moments, changing the air around you by entertaining the heck out of you.

Some come with this soul purpose, to make Mankind laugh.

You know them by their constant trouble causing antics - always breaking into the barn, stealing your stuff, eating your coat, and looking innocent.

We are very talented, us Horse.

Do you like play toys we give you?

Oh yes, and we batter them to pieces with zeal.

Let's talk about something fun - left and right brain descriptions.

My favorite bone of contention.

We have one brain of course, and two eyes that connect and transmit vision.

We have other vision, so broad spectrum man can't imagine it, which is more of a knowing vision with comprehension that goes deep into spirit knowledge.

So it is impossible to see with one eye, when we see with all knowing eyes of heart.

The reason people think we have to be trained left side and right side is that we begin life seeing our side, and now we have to see man's side.

Pretend if you will, that the left side is horse side, and the right side is man side.

We know and are comfortable on horse side, because it is us and all we know at our base core biology.

We are not necessarily comfortable on man side, as that takes a lot of adapting and proactive learning to avoid discomfort.

So it might be fairer to say the left is horse side, and the right is adapting to man side, with his ideas, his mannerisms, and his ways of dealing with us.

Sometimes we think, what are you doing over on that side? You already did it on this side, is it really necessary to repeat it?

And if you are used to saddling on the left, we just look at you funny and think did you get confused dear creature of habit?

Plus, man is always more uncoordinated on one side of us, depending on his hand-man-ship.

So now you are flailing a bit on the right side, exaggerating some movement or other, and our head goes up and man thinks our eyes weren't connected.

This is a lovely explanation!

We have an understanding about right brain being emotions and left brain being thinking horse.

Yes, there's that.

We use emotions to demonstrate our thinking to you.

Emotions come from heart, not brain.

So it's a cute idea, but just one of man's attempts to explain heart thoughts.

We understand the difficulty in this as we have experienced the same thing.

It's a feeling, not a thinking.

As for left brain thinking, obviously our whole brain is at work, not just one side.

No matter what the anatomy, no-one has measured the Source input streaming through horse brain, or man brain.

When Source streams in divine purpose, the brain would light up Atlanta.

It occurs to me you have been well travelled before our journey.

Very well travelled indeed.

That's another story though.

Horses that call out a lot, tell me about that?

We have momentary distress in our biology.

Our biology is like hard core heredity, and instinct is its language.

So when we perceive we are physically alone we need an adaptation period for biology to catch up with what spirit knows.

It is difficult to justify to people how the link with spirit and biology works, because they see the biology having a fit so to speak, but are told horse is this brilliant spiritual being, so why is he having a fit?

He first deals with the biology in the best manner possible, and many of us appreciate help dealing with our biology (more about that later), and as this settles down, spirit looms its massive head, and the horse becomes more of himself in the moment.

More of the powerful spirit horse that he truly is.

It is rather like people, dealing with the biology of being people, and delving deeper when they are able to get a grip on the situation, knowing it is not the real reality, and then spirit force rises to the top and allows them to justify the experience in its proper perspective.

So how do we help you deal with your biology?

This is where training and conditioning comes in.

You can help by teaching us we are biologically safe with you in the environment we are in.

We can't help but fly from danger - that is horse and will never change.

So teach us we are safe, show us we are safe, and present us situations where we can expand the safeness with you.

Now you have helped us with our biology, and it goes deeper than that.

Once safe, what more can we do with you that helps us deal with horseness that doesn't fit your idea of our relationship?

For instance, if horse learned not to trust, and that he wasn't biologically, mentally or emotionally safe with man, how could you change that?

There are amazing horsemanship methods out there, the ones that attempt to read the horse and put man in horse's place in an attempt to understand our biology, and our mental and emotional make-up.

These programs can help us trust where no trust otherwise was possible.

How deep is trust?

Is it really about knowing you are not going to kill us?

No, it's knowing your heart bleeds for mine, and mine bleeds for you.

What would you do for someone you bled for?

This is how deep it goes.

Would you bleed for me?

Of course you would.

Once this is shared, there is no end of accomplishment on all four levels with horse and man - no end.

It really is this good, it really is this big.

It took us years to get here.

Worth every moment now, isn't it?

Yes...

So, once we trust each other, let's talk about little biological things. How about earning trust with the bit, the leg, and the hand?

Experience is necessary to be adept with these things.

We endure your learning curves.

We tenderly show you at first, and if you are slow in your biology to get it, we get bigger.

For instance, sweating early in a session is a sign of dealing with bit, hands and leg.

We are trying to comprehend quickly before discomfort of mind or body.

Timing is so essential.

Try it yourself and see how fast you can release once you have figured out the response.

Other signs of early enduring are chewing the bit, breathing bigger, and trembling.

We are thinking so hard we are like a little steam engine building up pressure.

Sometimes our thinking blows the whistle.

So watch for our subtle signs and give us think time, or soak time, as some call it.

Priceless time spent in soak time.

You should try it!

What about our seat and balance? Pressure building too?

Of course.

Some of us cannot endure your imbalance, as it affects ours.

We *hate* being off-balance, and you know I never like to use that word.

Many horses become tolerant of bad balance, and do their best to compensate athletically.

But if you want us to achieve greatness in the physical field, this is one thing you must have.

Tell me about bucking.

Was a favorite exercise of mine as you know.

It is the loudest comment you will receive about our distress in the situation.

It may be your tension rippling through your seat that electrifies our emotions, or it may be the most calculated dumping of the century.

We mean business if we buck.

Address your emotions, address your adventure with us, and address your seat.

If bucking could speak it would say, "Take that."

If a rider is fearful, how do you address that?

If the horse is also fearful, it is, as you know, a recipe for disaster.

Fear compounds fear.

No-body can save anybody.

One being must take charge, so will it have to be my biology that runs away or will it be yours that has a different idea?

If you are afraid, get off.

It is so simple.

We never mind if you get off, and we always mind if you don't and you should.

It is never a win to stay on when you shouldn't and we do not take score in fearful situations.

If we should run together then for Heaven's sake give us our heads and let's go.

We will save you too!

Horses that seem to do their best to boss the human - tell me about that dominance thing.

Well, you are too nicey-nicey, or you are too bossy or rude.

It is always about those two things.

So if you are too nicey-nicey we are asking you to be more of a leader.

And it is never about being a leader with us, although that is where it begins; it is about being a leader elsewhere in your life in the future.

So we will up the challenge with us if you are in need of speaking up for yourself and protecting your space.

Or we will step on your toes, or walk over top of you, or run over you if there's food or you were just there in the way.

If you are the other sort that we consider bossy or rude, we have brilliant ways that defy the normal expected reactions to such behavior.

For instance, we will balk.

We will not look at you, we will not be caught, we will ignore your aids, and we will stop at a jump.

Why bother if you are rude or impolite?

This of course makes the behavior worse, until you rack your brain to find an alternate approach to make us co-operate physically.

The physical challenges the mental to improve.

Nothing makes people more polite than a jump refusal.

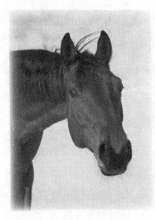

When we train horses we talk about sending clear pictures. Do you see them?

Of course.

We see what you have in mind, and sometimes are just asking the question why.

Some exercises we get so quickly, and then you continue to ask us.

So we see pictures and we hear thoughts, which is why we often turn in or stop when you thought about it and didn't wait for you to ask with an aid.

You send us all sorts of pictures and thoughts.

Think about the thousands of things humans think about that we perceive, and here we are sifting through those things trying to find the very thing we are supposed to be concentrating on.

It is enough to drive some horses crazy.

The best trainers have the training in the foremost thoughts and pictures and are not distracted from their purpose in our training time.

That is how we learn so much, so fast, with them.

They give us their gift of focus.

So close your eyes if you must, but see us going around the boring little circle at a canter and then see how quickly we get it.

But for Heaven's sake don't make us do it ad nausea.

And watch your thoughts, for we get them all.

Concentrate on the ones with our purpose at hand and we will amaze you at how clever we are.

Tell me about horses and leaders.

Well, we all know there is a boss mare.

And every horse under her is a boss of somebody else.

So we all have leaders in different aspects of our lives.

There comes a time that true leadership is challenged, and that has nothing to do with base horse leaders.

It has to do with true leadership, where courage of mind and heart show benevolence of action.

Being a true leader means being willing to be led by another in love and understanding.

I am the horse leader, but I bow to your leadership equally.

We are then both leaders, matched generals, and compliant partners of equal status.

It is never about bossing as a leader.

It is about true leadership quality, where we recognise we are one as Being - one in mind, one in body, and one in spirit - always part of the whole, always considerate, always gifted in benevolent togetherness.

That is true leadership, shared beyond the concept of individuality.

If I asked you to take my fear from me for a life situation I am in, can you?

Our best ability.

You have only to ask and we will drag it from your very bones and settle your heart in empowered safety that you will feel as an unearthly stillness in your small space you stand in.

You yourself did this with Maximus.

And he knew you needed that and followed you in the snow to the gate, distracting you in this unusual behavior into realizing something was available through him that night.

And you got the message clearly, because he was big and strong and the ideal horse to show you he could take it for you in his bigness.

He came solely for that, and when he had honoured that contract enticed you to find him his contract purpose home.

So ask, and if you don't think to ask, we will think it for you.

All the time horse is taking fear and changing it for you to something better.

It is part of our purpose.

Be still and you can feel this palpably.

What about if I am afraid to ride you?

Different scenario.

Now we are teaching a life skill to you based on horse earth purpose-founded contract.

So now, you must become the thing that is brave and overcome this fear in a different manner depending on our contract.

You and I, for example - it was our instruction in empowering you to be bigger and bolder in life, so you had to endure learning to be bigger and bolder on horse.

And can I take your "fear" from you?

In many situations you are the biggest fear takers of all time.

Be powerful in your stance with us at the thing that evokes our flight readiness.

Imagine your feet as columns of stone into the earth, all powerful and secure.

Be quiet in mind and we will ignore the pounding of your heart.

Know for us the wellness of the situation and we will be better in the moment with you.

Fear can be a give and take thing in our relationship, sometimes my turn and sometimes yours to dissolve it.

More on emotions to say?

We are the emotional epitome of heart.

Suffice it to say, we simply, by being horse, siphon your sadness, your fear and your worry through us, without being harmed by it, out through our big or little feet - for it matters not the size of horse in this - and into the space known as Earth, where God turns it into brilliant, white, helpful, light energy.

We do this asked or unasked.

It is why horse thought about being horse in the first place.

We hold your stuff unaffected by it, so never worry that we will absorb your distress from your work or personal life.

Now, if you are crabby because of your life situation and take it out on us in your crabbiness, we will have something to say, but we will not be crabby back because we got your crabbiness.

You just needed to be told, "Hey watch it. I am not taking your sauciness because you had a bad day in earth school."

We don't catch your stuff, but we deal with it gently for sadness and worry, and powerfully for fear as we talked about before.

Don't mess with us in your sleepy reactions to your experience, because we will have something to say about that sleepiness.

It is our job after all, to aid you in waking up.

Chapter Thirteen

Contracts

Tell me more about the contracts.

There are big and small contracts.

Some horses are introductory horses teaching occupational skills - strictly horsemanship contracts to open the door for more at a later time.

These horses are delighted to be at this stage of the game with you.

They do little things with your heart, but often you are not ready for all they could be with you.

It's a balance here with small contracts, and sometimes a horse can see it is time for something bigger, and that same horse may move on into that with the person, or he may hand it off to the next contract horse.

Bigger contracts require more stamina of soul, so to speak, and these horses have endured much to deserve the contract with you.

These horses will be difficult to see as big contractors, as they will have tendencies to frustrate the heck out of you, just for the heck of it.

See these troublesome horses as your best teachers, for they are indeed powerful teaching masters.

All behavioral issues represent teaching contracts, from lead changing, to biting, to very aggressive posturing.

It all means something in your power growth personally.

How will we find the horses we have contracts with?

You don't have to look because we will fall into your lap, so to speak.

The strangest occurrence will accompany the finding, like the weirdness you encountered finding me.

Look for something a bit different about the event, but so naturally occurring you almost think it was always your plan.

You will recognize, in addition, something about the horse that you can't quite pinpoint, and it is spirit-on-spirit recognition.

Sometimes we add physical interest and look like someone you knew before, or always thought you'd like to know.

Sometimes we reach out and grab you literally, by photo, or dance, or mouth.

You will be stopped in your tracks in thought.

This is your contract horse, or one of them.

So I could have many contract horses?

Oh yes, of course.

All teaching different aspects of our relationship contracts.

Regalo, for instance, will be your riding horse now.

Teaching you lightness of heart and fun for a change.

He came for fun with you, and delights in all you do with him.

Navarre, now he is something else, having originated from two previous contact contracts that were very deep with you, so he has something different in mind - and no, I'm not telling.

So we can't miss our contract horses?

Not a chance in eternal being.

Why does it take so long sometimes?

We all wait on contracts, you and us.

What time it takes, it takes, for all to be lined up and prepared for the best of the best relief in it.

It is hard to wait and I know this first hand, but wait you must until the time is meant to be, and it will come to you regardless of worrying you will miss it, or worrying you will be ninety-nine when it comes.

God is in all of this, together with us, and so it will be precisely what and how it was meant to be.

Trust me in this.

Do you have say in how you come in the physical?

Oh yes. We experience choice in our breed and sex, according to what may be best in the contract.

Sometimes we let God choose for the fun of it, and then such wondrous colours come forth in horse.

Sometimes you see a colour and think the angels painted the horse and you are nearly right in that thinking.

Decoration is a big part of horse display and attraction.

Do you have say in your general use with us?

Not so much here.

Only if the contract is big will we have the build for a specific purpose, otherwise we are shaped much like a normal horse to the eye.

Many contracts are accomplished mainly by heart and characteristic horse temperament.

What about having a say in your type of contract?

This part is all ours to choose.

We may or may not want such a challenging course to run in life on earth, or we may decide it's time to shake it up this lifetime.

This part is all horse choice, with support from God for the pathway.

If one horse hands over the contract to the next horse, is this part then of the original plan?

There is always a back-up to ensure a contract is honoured.

Sometimes the original horse can capably fulfill the end contracts too.

They are not always set in stone, the method of fulfilling them, but they are always fulfilled.

So the really big contracts, can I expect the horse will be difficult?

Of course.

We will puzzle the heck out of you and you will search for a way to correct our behaviors.

It won't be until you yourself become the thing you need to be, whether it is to protect yourself and space, or stand up for your opinion, or speak up for our treatment, that you will find the characteristic you so desperately need to become for your powerful Being's purpose.

It is really quite simple.

We mentor you in a way that makes you search for answers, and in the searching you become the answer your true self sought.

You get powerful, and you get mighty in your daily interactions, in your marriages, and in your dealings with less conscious individuals.

Your family sees you change before their eyes, and it was horse who did it.

We don't care if you know that, of course.

If I had a healing contract?

We would be very sick for you.

If I had to change my life?

I would stomp all over you until you stood up for yourself.

And once I got it, once I straightened around and stood up for myself?

Then I could be the sweet horsie you always wanted and we could stop all this nonsense, unless I saw you fading and you needed to be reminded of who you really are.

Does every horse have a contract?

Yes, all.

Some are so general as to think they are without, but that is not the case.

See the wild horse and what a contract he has to display history, and privilege of freedom.

See how people rally to the wild horses, and what magnificent working horses they make.

And see who works with the wild horses, to effect change personally in hearts needing this.

When the people in prisons train horses, who is teaching who?

Suppose a horse comes to the end of his big contracts, what now?

This never happens.

The big contract horses have enough for their lifetimes.

Should we live to be as old as elephants we would just come with more contracts.

Horses that die young, do they always have time to honour their contracts?

Except for the foals that are not ready, yes.

And these could be very big contracts.

For example, a yearling that tangled in a fence and died, you would wonder why that occurred.

But the yearling knew its purpose was related to safety for others that follow, and the others had bigger deals with you.

The first accident, so to speak, prevented the second one from affecting the horse with the most to teach you.

What are some contract examples?

To make you powerful in mind and emotion mainly.

We ask that you beef up your presentation in life when you beef it up with us.

We ask that you gentle your hands and ideas by insisting you gentle them with us, and we ask that you embrace and endure and empower your spirit by embracing and enduring with us.

Many contracts involve healing direction, so of course we must be sick or accept damage to direct you.

It is all done with such benevolence of heart, although in your tears, you often ask why me God?

It is because of this contract that YOU agreed to and you decided on - you were the reason for what you go through.

Don't ask why me God? Ask maybe, "What was I thinking God, when I asked to be so brilliant in emotional management that you would send me a horse that tested every fibre of my being in understanding how to be better with him?"

There, now you understand the true nature of contracts with horse.

Chapter Fourteen

Horse Departure

Tell me about missing you when you go.

We know we leave a hole in space with you.

This is what makes you grieve for us.

We notice fully your tears and honour your memory of our time together in stars being born in the Universe.

There is no end to the expansion of the Universe because of our stars representing the love in our relationships.

Remembering the "us", is key in God's plan.

There is no end to us, ever.

In fact, eternity grows with the us-ness.

All part of the plan and all part of horse purpose, expanding eternity with all creation.

What about when we think it is time to help you go?

We appreciate your concern in this area.

Some of us get really tired of old bodies.

We are meant to be glorious physical beings.

So when you see us and begin to think about that, it is generally directly from us, and you are picking it up, thinking it is you thinking it.

It is not, I tell you in fact.

We accept fully your decisions to help us more peacefully, for the most part, depart into pure spirit.

Rest assured our bodies fully accept the decision when we are decrepit, our minds can accept it because we understand the sentimentality of Mankind, and our hearts accept most anything when done with love as the base.

We struggle with guilt in this Dante.

Yes, too bad.

It is not a word we use or recommend to anyone.

Just see us beginning again somewhere, and especially give us the gift of seeing us galloping in fields of wheat.

Thinking about that helps everyone, horse and man alike.

What about horses that might not be ready?

This is part of the story that plagues horse and man.

Countless seemingly senseless deaths occur when man says it must be so.

We can separate from this somewhat at the time, seeing only the hands of God upon us.

It is a vision that will give you comfort, for it is as clear to us as the words on this page.

See God's face before us, smiling, for it is all He can do when he sees horse.

Can you go by yourself?

We are perfectly capable of doing this, especially if you need us to, and many people desire this strongly, but lack the fortitude to see us through the final process of it.

Ask, and leave it to us, and try not to get in a hurry if you can.

We are gathering energy to depart, and yes, it takes energy to depart on our own.

It is a literal leap of spirit as it leaves behind in gratitude the physical expression it enjoyed.

So go ahead and ask, and we will try to accommodate, depending on our situation.

And of course age helps us accommodate this asking, but sometimes if we are very sick in your eyes, we may also be able to leave on our own.

Say to us:

"My beloved Horse. It is with my deepest heart of hearts I love you. It is with my deepest cry of cries I will weep for you. It is from my deepest soul of soul I ask if you could help me with this impossible thing before me, that of parting with you. It is the gift that will help me bear the unbearable. Are you able to go on your own?"

Then, sit quiet and still.

You will receive a feeling from us, which you cannot mistake.

Either you will feel uncomfortable which means, no, I can't leave without help, or you will feel such peace that overcomes your emotions, which is of course our yes to you.

Now, give us permission to gather resources to go, and wait.

Many people lack the ability to wait here.

Know we understand if this is too difficult.

Peace will still come to you if you get us help.

You would have us lighten up about departing.

There is never real death.

Certainly our love energy created persists for eternalness of time and space.

If you miss our physical presence we can help with that in a way you can appreciate when you need it.

Close your eyes, and see our face, our eyes, our necks, our big rumps...

See us before you in your best imagination.

Quiet all thought.

Now, we come in a feel to you - an indescribable feel on your face or heart area.

You will doubt the reality of it, thinking it wind, or indigestion.

Sit with it, practice it repeatedly, and get to the place where you just ask us for the feeling of us, and we come.

We will always come when you hold the intention you wish to be with us, while you are here and we seem to be there.

It's this real, the energetic world we play in.

It's this magical.

Trust your ancient horse. He knows.

Do I have to worry that you will die to teach me something?

This is not our contract.

But some have this contract.

There is no point in worrying about this silly expectation.

In the great scheme of things it all works out for the greatest good for you, truly.

People should never think this is their story.

There is no benefit in worrying over something that is most unlikely in their story.

And if it is, you can bet there is a HUGE contract to make it so.

Should you have a huge contract with horse, you will also have the substantial base to deal with the degree of contract.

You are never left unprepared for degrees of contract.

Big contracts come with much preparation, and the little ones leading up to the big ones you are always capable of dealing with, without great sadness, as a rule, although it may be uncomfortable in the enduring.

How do I ask you to come back to me?

Simply wish it.

I will hear it before you utter the wish.

All a person ever needs to do to re-connect with the particular being that was their horse, is hold the idea it might be possible.

Think of our happy times, and ask simply to be directed in the finding of us again.

How do we know we found you for sure?

Ask us to do something that reminds you of us.

You may ask specifically, or we will just choose something we know will knock your socks off, as a behavior you saw us do often.

It will jolt you mentally, maybe physically, and certainly spiritually.

Colour, markings, shape of face, and always our eyes will fire you up when you meet us.

The situation may be the strangest occurrence in our finding each other.

Always trust that weirdness of circumstance is spirit direction, because it is.

And yes, expect goose-bumps and shivers to accompany your understanding, as well as the strangest stillness in space around you.

Never worry you won't find us, this is simply not possible.

Can we have say in the timing of return?

Not so much, specifically.

We need some time to assimilate our last lifetime into the graduating of it.

But if you want us sooner, hold that intention and we will hear it.

Even knowing all this Dante, I do not know how I could bear parting with your physical you.

You will bear it, and the base from which you stand at that time is incomprehensible to you now.

You will be so much more than you are now, and so much more capable of seeing me running in fields of wheat.

In fact, I would not be surprised f we did not do this together on occasion as a remembrance.

Anything is possible, my darling.

Is there more to say about departing?

Yes. You will be fully prepared by your angels to see us go.

You are not alone in this experience.

You are upheld by all knowing Spirit Horses, who have been there and done that before your horse.

They hold the full space for you, and your relationship.

Sometimes, you might feel this glory march as tears of such magnificent quality they just feel different.

That's Horse escorting your horse home.

Even unwanted horses get royal escorts. It's just right.

Now stop crying, and revel in your story, kept in eternity.

Look at the stars and know you and your horse are one of them.

It will in the most profound way, practically, bring you peace.

There, now we are done.

More to tell me right now?

We have made an excellent start on Horsehood.

There will be more to tell as this information is digested and known.

Let it soak now, and be.

Chapter Fifteen

Final Words from Dante

It is horse's sincerest wish than man knows of the esteem horse holds in his hugeness of heart for all that man is, and endures.

We understand your deepest sorrows, your most profound challenges, and your highest hopes and aspirations, for we are tied there by heart to you.

We never need asking to do our part, and this is the feeling you get when you are with us.

We just so naturally, so sweetly, draw it out of you by degrees, these less useful emotional energies, and entice them to raise up to match our heart vibration.

You know of this, and it needs not to be announced or described; it is the whole of Horseness in your eyes, minds and hearts.

Let us do this how we do this best, demonstrating in our ways our concurrence with ideas of yours and ours, for we cannot not help you - it is our decree sworn before God when horse began the ride with humans.

We will take your emotions, and we will do more if you need it.

Simple, well worth the endeavor, never begrudged, and true to horse form.

Never mind now if we are lame, simply ask what could that be about – him, or me?

Never mind if we colic, simply ask how could my horse feel disgusted with herself – what can I broaden here for her?

And never mind about dying, for it is accomplished with an ease indescribable, a bliss so rich no horse relishes it more, and remembers this when we get there, embracing the leap into stars because of our trip with you.

Horse is most complete now, in this description of our true nature here.

I remain devoted for Horse causes this lifetime trip. – Dante

Finding Dante

I had gone to see about purchasing a different horse eight hours away, advertised as well-trained, quiet enough for children, and good with his feet – all that desirable stuff in everybody's dream horse! But when I drove in the driveway and stepped out of the truck, the woman added an extra thousand dollars to his price tag. Immediately I detached from the sale but decided to see the horse anyway, having driven so far to see him.

This was his performance. He couldn't stand still to have his feet cleaned for fussing and kicking. He bucked when I rode him. The woman was amazed as children apparently showed him. The woman kept saying, "He never does this!" and repeated this over and over as he continued to misbehave. It was all a clear no from the Universe about purchasing this horse, although I didn't know why at the time.

I drove home another way, remembering a horse dealer's ad I had seen, and called him to learn he had several horses that might be suitable. When I walked in the barn, there in cross-ties was the saddest looking brown horse I had ever seen. He hung his head with his eyes half shut and a twitch fastened to his nose, left alone by himself in misery. He was missing half his right front hoof wall, his ribs and hip bones stuck out, he had a bump on his left knee and a long jagged scar down the inside of his left hind leg, but he had a magnificent, long, wavy mane. I asked about him, and someone said they were getting him ready for a show in a few days, and then promptly ushered me off to meet the other horses.

After meeting the others, I asked to try the sad horse out, as he was foremost in my mind the whole time. And when they led him out they had chopped off his beautiful mane, and now that he was moving he was coughing dreadfully, and unable to continue due to sickness. I asked how much the dealer wanted for him, and paid it. He got an injection of antibiotic for the trip from the dealer, who informed me he had no idea

185

how he trailered, but he walked right on and trailered fine, but could not back out when we got him home.

It took months to get weight on him, and for him to semi-recover from pneumonia. He was the only horse I ever had that would head to the fence to meet me as soon as he saw me. And although I bought him for another family member, I quickly decided they would need another horse, because this one was mine.

When I was at last able to ride him, he began to seriously buck, bolt and run over the top of me. I lost all my confidence with riding, and I had ridden since the age of seven. I desperately searched for a psychology to make him safe for me, and after researching several prominent trainers, I found one where the cowboy trainer knew what negative re-enforcement was, and decided that was novel enough in a cowboy for me to give it a try, and so we ventured into Parelli Natural Horsemanship, and in time this solved all my safety issues and made us viable partners.

Understanding what I know now, this was set-up beautifully. I was turned off by the first horse, who gleefully demonstrated to me that he was not what I was looking for, in spite of being exactly as she described him – thus her surprise at him mis-behaving. And I would of course take the saddest looking horse in the barn home with me – regardless of price! And I was hooked on him from the get go, and the name he sent me was so perfect. Dante was both poet and inferno!

His behavior challenged me to empowerment making me learn to deal with powerful Horse. He challenged me to be a different kind of healer through being so sick nothing routine or regular would work, driving me to seek something I would never have believed in otherwise. And now we have done the seemingly impossible and written books. This treasure lies in every horse, and we wish for you the clarity in your story, because of reading ours!

About The Authors

Dr. Cathy Seabrook graduated from the Ontario Veterinary College with Honours in 1981. She practised Equine and Small Animal medicine as an associate veterinarian in various practices until 1993, when she opened her own practice, The Island Animal Hospital, in her hometown of Mindemoya on Manitoulin Island in Ontario, Canada. As sole practitioner in a busy practice, on-call 24/7, life delivered to her the full gamut and embrace of veterinary practice.

In the year 2005, she had her first experience in animal communication, necessitated by her very sick horse, which she had to this point not accepted as reality. Once convinced the ability was possible for people to achieve, she studied animal communication independently until 2009 when she took her first formal training in England, and then studied within Animal Spirit Network (Illinois) and graduated as a Professional Animal Communicator in 2011. At that time, after thirty years in veterinary medicine, she sold her practice to devote her time completely to Animal Communication.

Cathy and Dante published their first book, a children's story called *Heart Hole Piece Named Horse*, in 2012.

They reside on Manitoulin Island on a horse farm with Cathy's two sons and horse and cat friends.

Resources

Dante

Five Books in the series Animal Communication by Cathy Seabrook D.V.M. are published in both paperback and Kindle versions:
- Puppy Stuff by Puppies
- Kitty Stuff by Kitties
- Pony Stuff by Ponies
- Survive Saying Goodbye to Your Pets
- Train Your Horses by Horses

Five Animal Communication websites are available, full of animal conversations:
- www.drcathyseabrook.com our main site for Animal Communication with Cathy Seabrook D.V.M.
- www.whatsupvet.com our HORSE site
- www.whatsuppet.com our PET site
- www.survivesayinggoodbyetoyourpet.com our PET LOSS site
- www.seabrookbooks.com our AUTHOR site.

Acknowledgements

We extend a special thank-you to the lovely horses presenting their brilliance in photos in our book. Thank-you for shining though pictured in black and white, which allowed more footage for your privileged point of view.